A POETRY PRIMER

by

GERALD SANDERS

PROFESSOR OF ENGLISH
MICHIGAN STATE NORMAL COLLEGE
YPSILANTI, MICHIGAN

HOLT, RINEHART & WINSTON
New York

AUGUST, 1960

PREFACE

THIS book is designed to help students in the early stages of their study, when poetry is like something behind locked doors for which they have no key. It is meant to be helpful particularly in introductory courses where considerable poetry is read, and where, without devoting too much time to this, students are required to know something of the elements of prosody. It is written simply, therefore, in the hope that once it is in the hands of students, they can teach themselves; it makes little effort to consider matters of chief interest to the advanced student and the critic; and it introduces no innovations. It might be well if all the teachers and critics and writers of poetry would meet and settle once for all the questions of poetic and prosodic terminology, probably scrapping the present terminology, and even the present system of teaching prosody. But in view of the swiftness with which proponents and opponents of any small change rush to battle, it is unlikely that such a convention will be held this year; and until it is held, it seems best to employ the terms used for some hundreds of years without material damage to the quality of English poetry or to its appreciation by those not writing it.

Experience shows that many students need to know not only something about rhythm and metre and stanzas and feet, but how to read a poem intelligently. I have, therefore, added a very elementary section, included so far as I know in no handbook of this sort, on how to study the content of a poem. And I have tried to deal as fully as possible in so short a work with such troublesome forms as the sonnet, the ode, and free verse, in order to make these as clear as possible to students.

For helpful comments on the manuscript, I am indebted to Professors Alma Blount, C. F. Harrold, and H. W. Reninger; and for permission to use some of their verse to illustrate a number of forms, to a number of my former students.

TABLE OF CONTENTS

CHAPTER I

THE POET

It is not the office of this book to account for the poetic gift or to explain the processes of the poetic mind; for it is not necessary to understand the poet's nature to appreciate his product, or to know how poetry is created to like it.[1] Yet to have some elementary knowledge of the poet may aid the student in understanding poetry itself.

In the first place, the poet has an exquisitely sensitive mind that makes him alive to *nuances* that escape the average person. He is aware of nice distinctions in both the inner and outer worlds —nature and the mind—and apprehends subtle influences that pass unheeded by prosaic folk. Bits of knowledge, inappreciable experiences, evanescent emotions of which a blunter consciousness is scarcely cognizant, he seizes upon and uses. Thus he is often able to trace more obscure causes and to perceive more distant effects than others usually do.

He also has a fine memory—not perhaps for names and telephone numbers, but for whatever he has experienced of action and emotion in the world around him or in his own mind. Wordsworth, for instance, says that poetry "takes its origin from emotion *recollected* in tranquillity."[2] But to the average person such experiences tend to recede with the passing of time and to become nebulous and indistinct. The poet, on the other hand, seems able long after the event to recall his experience and reproduce an emotion with the same acute consciousness as when they were new.

He has a wider and more varied experience than most men— the result, first, of his great sensitivity; secondly, of his ability to observe man and nature closely; and thirdly, of a deep sympathy, which enables him to enter easily into the experiences of others. Nothing seems too great or too small for his attention. He is, it is true, chiefly preoccupied with the mystery men call death, with

[1] Many books and articles, a number by poets themselves, deal with these subjects, and a list of some of the more important ones is given in the bibliography at the end of this work.

[2] Preface to *Lyrical Ballads*. The italics are mine.

[1]

beauty becoming dust or living on, with love and its ways with men, and with man's eternal warfare with the demons of the mind; yet, like Autolycus in Shakespeare's *Winter's Tale,* he is a snapper-up of unconsidered trifles too; and has time to note how the daffodils "come before the swallow dares, and take the winds of March with beauty," how a crow shakes down the dust of snow from a hemlock tree, how the finger of a dead baby seems to cling to the hand performing the last rites on the little body, and how on dusty city streets one unaccountably hears lake water lapping with low sounds on the shore.

Further, he possesses in an extraordinary degree the ability to integrate his wide experience. By means of a powerful imagination, which acts upon the jumbled mass of information in his mind, he is able to create new experiences, to combine incongruous elements in such way as to produce harmonious effects, and from old ideas to secure new connotations.

In addition he has the happy faculty of expressing his ideas and emotions in adequate images. This is one of his rarest attributes, for the expression of emotionalized experience in fitting language is the culmination of man's ability to communicate, and in this the poet is supreme. Let two examples, chosen from among hundreds that might be cited, illustrate this faculty. When Shakespeare wishes to show the power of love to lift the spirit of one sunk in misery and surrounded by misfortune, he says:

> When in disgrace with fortune and men's eyes,
> I all alone beweep my outcast state,
> And trouble deaf heaven with my bootless cries,
> And look upon myself, and curse my fate . . .
> Haply I think on thee, and then my state
> Like to the lark at break of day arising
> From sullen earth, sings hymns at heaven's gate.

And Herrick, being concerned with the passing of beauty and the transitoriness of life, seizes upon the image of the daffodil, and uses its beauty and brief existence to make tangible his thought:

> Fair daffodils, we weep to see
>   You haste away so soon:
> As yet the early-rising sun
>   Has not attained his noon.
>   Stay, stay
>   Until the hasting day
>   Has run

But to the even-song;
And, having prayed together, we
Will go with you along.

We have short time to stay, as you,
We have as short a spring;
As quick a growth to meet decay
As you, or anything.
We die,
As your hours do, and dry
Away,
Like to the summer's rain;
Or as the pearls of morning's dew
Ne'er to be found again.

And with his other gifts, the poet is endowed with a fine sense for melody and form, which guides him in selecting the proper pattern for his thought. Thus he is able to wed sense and sound in such way that good poetry always gives us the impression that for any one idea the form in which it is wrought is that alone which can give us the highest satisfaction. The poet has the same delight in grouping words to give beautiful and striking effects that an artist has in grouping colors, and a musician in arranging sounds; and this delight conveys itself in the form of his poetry, so that form and idea become inseparable.

This list of the endowments of a poet is not meant to be complete, but it will serve to introduce the poet to the student, who as he proceeds in his studies will himself find many other attributes. Nor is it meant to infer that these belong to the poet alone. In some degree all men possess at least part of them, and creative writers other than poets may possess some of them in high degree; but in the poet they all meet, and it is in him that they are most fully developed.

CHAPTER II

THE NATURE AND USES OF POETRY

POETRY is emotionalized experience. It is universal truth in thought or feeling, transmuted by the imagination into fitting images, and expressed in beautiful, and usually patterned, language. It is the perfect expression of a worthy idea in measured language. It is the product when a brooding imagination finds in man and nature deep matter for consideration and transmits its findings to others for their delight and edification.

These and many other things—more prosaic or more imaginative—may be said of poetry by way of describing or explaining it, yet none is in any real sense a definition; for poetry, in common with such other abstract things as art, beauty, love, and nature, cannot be defined once and for all. It is, in the first place, too complex and varied to be narrowed to the limits of a single definition. Men's ideas of what is poetry, moreover, change from age to age, while different men in the same age do not always think alike about it, as the following comments show.

Poesy . . . is an art of imitation . . . a speaking picture, with this end,—to teach and delight.
—SIR PHILIP SIDNEY, *The Defence of Poesy*, 1595

Poetry is the art of uniting pleasure with beauty by calling imagination to the help of reason.
—SAMUEL JOHNSON, *Life of Milton*, 1781

Poetry is the spontaneous overflow of powerful feelings.
—WORDSWORTH, Preface to *Lyrical Ballads*, 1800

A poem is that species of composition, which is opposed to works of science, by proposing for its *immediate* object pleasure, not truth; and from all other species—(having *this* object in common with it)—it is discriminated by proposing to itself such delight from the *whole,* as is compatible with a distinct gratification from each component part.
—COLERIDGE, *Biographia Literaria*, XIV, 1817

Poetry is the language of the imagination and the passions . . . the universal language which the heart holds with nature and itself . . . an

imitation of nature . . . the high-wrought enthusiasm of fancy and feeling.
—WILLIAM HAZLITT, "On Poetry in General," 1818

Poetry is the record of the best and happiest moments of the happiest and best minds.

—SHELLEY, *A Defence of Poetry*, 1840

Poetry is the utterance of a passion for truth, beauty, and power, embodying and illustrating its conceptions by imagination and fancy, and modulating its language on the principle of variety and uniformity. Its means are whatever the universe contains, and its ends pleasure and exaltation.

—LEIGH HUNT, "What Is Poetry" in *Imagination and Fancy*, 1844

I would define, in brief, the poetry of words as *the Rhythmical Creation of Beauty*.

—POE, "The Poetic Principle," 1850

[Poetry is] nothing less than the most perfect speech of man, that in which he comes nearest to being able to utter the truth.
—MATTHEW ARNOLD, "Wordsworth" in *Essays in Criticism*, Second Series, 1888 [1]

But if it is not possible to define poetry exactly, we may nevertheless discover some of its qualities and reach some conclusion as to its nature. And this is sufficient until one becomes a mature student of poetry, when he may formulate his own definition, with the assurance that if his studies have been sincere his definition will be satisfactory, at least for himself.

The most obvious distinction to make concerning poetry is between it and prose. Such distinction at first seems apparent. A child who has barely learned to read may distinguish between them by the appearance of each on the page. A maturer student learns, however, that such a simple test is not always reliable, since it offers no help when listening to something read aloud; or when poetry from another language is translated into prose, as in the *Psalms*, parts of the Old Testament prophecies, and many Greek poems; or in some modern free verse, where the page arrangement resembles closely that of prose. But if mere appearance is not always trustworthy as a means of distinguishing poetry from prose, other distinctions exist that will help. One is the tendency of poetry to resolve itself into patterns and to assume regular cadences, while

---

[1] These dates are of publication. Sidney, for instance, wrote his comment about 1581, Shelley his in 1821. But the dates are close enough to give an idea of the approximate time at which each was stated.

prose in general seeks to avoid these. Another is the tendency to establish a harmony of sounds in poetry—words, and even the letters which form words, being chosen to give concord and melody—while the writer of prose avoids a too mellifluous flow of words. But not only in structure is poetry distinguishable from prose; it differs also in aim. The primary appeal of prose is to the reason, of poetry to the emotions and the imagination.

Yet the boundaries between the two are not absolute, and there are frequent shadings of one into the other. It is difficult, for instance, for one listening to certain passages read aloud to say which are meant as poetry and which as prose. There is, indeed, prosaic poetry in the works of the most illustrious poets, and poetic prose in the writings of those who make no pretence at being poets; yet it is usually easy to determine, by its context or in some other simple way, what to call such matter, without becoming involved in the disputes of mature critics over questionable passages. Occasionally, however, it may not be readily apparent in which category something belongs; and when this is true, one must seek the intention of the author and defer to this.[2] But as compared with the great body of prose and poetry that can be distinguished without difficulty, this borderland material is small, and such questions as arise over what to call it may safely be left to mature critics.

Another distinction, more difficult and more important, is that between poetry and mere verse [3]—more difficult because the difference has little to do with form but depends on a number of subjective qualities; and more important because on a student's ability to make such distinction depends his eventual intellectual status. This ability to distinguish between real poetry and mere writing in rime does not come in a day, however, but is the result of conscious study or long reading of good poetry, or both. Of these, reading is the more important; but having an intelligent idea of what are some of the marks of a good poem will help.

One important mark is the presence of an imaginative element. An evidence of this is the ability of the poet to interpret old matter

[2] An instance is Amy Lowell's *Can Grande's Castle,* which is more poetic than some of her work which she labels poetry; but her statement that she intended this as an experiment in prose should probably prevent our considering it as poetry.

[3] Some critics object to the terms *poetry* and *verse* as used in this sense, preferring that the adjectives *good* or *bad* be used to distinguish the quality of a poem. The reason this is not done here is to avoid the confusion which may result from the different connotations of *bad.* If the terms are understood, it is probably unimportant which are used; what is important is that the student should know the difference between the two classes.

[6]

in new ways, to re-present pictures of objects which have come within his experience in such way as to throw into prominence details unnoticed by us before, or to give us new delight in things with which we have so long been familiar that we have lost our relish for them.   Another evidence is the way in which the poet combines unlike images and feelings to form new ones, thus extending the bounds of his experience, and consequently bringing new experiences to us.   And still another evidence is the way in which from actual creations he develops ideal ones.   Although the poet is under the same obligation as the scientist to adhere to truth, the laws under which he works are not exacting in the same manner; hence results his advantage of being able to project his thought into realms beyond the jurisdiction of the ordinary seeker after truth, and to arrive at conclusions before others do.   This transcending of the actual and apparent, and approaching the ideal, results from the play of the imagination and is a test of good poetry.

Another mark of poetry is the presence of the emotional element.   Feeling an experience acutely, and wishing to create in his reader the same depth of feeling which he has, the poet associates certain emotions with the experience to give it vividness and thus make it produce the reaction he wishes.   It is this emotionalizing of experience which makes poetry at times richer than many find actual life, and helps men find in poetry a satisfaction which ordinary existence does not always give.   It is in the use of the emotional element that poetry differs chiefly from prose, for although emotion is present in prose, it is there properly subordinated to reason, while in poetry it is one of the dominant elements.   And in this respect also poetry differs from mere verse, for when a piece of writing depicts an emotion which gives the sense of being false, when it is mawkish or overdone, when it does not carry the reader with it, it cannot lay claim to real merit.

Another characteristic is the emphasis on beauty.   So much, indeed, is this a mark of poetry that it is possible to say that the chief end of poetry is to resolve the uncouth, the unfinished, the unseemly, and the inartistic into harmony and beauty.   It is doubtless because he feels the ugliness of a society that allows the poor to be ground down, the weak to be exploited by the strong, and life made unlovely for little children that the poet is so often interested in social conditions.   Likewise his preoccupation with the passing of youth, the transitoriness of life, the inevitability of death, and the mutability of nature is the result of his worship of beauty, his

[7]

desire for the permanency of loveliness, and his sorrow at the changes wrought by time and death. It should be noted, however, that although the poet as a rule uses sensuous language and beautiful images, he may at times resort to the grotesque and ugly; but even when he does this it is to give in the end a final effect of beauty. Thus in Spenser's *Faerie Queene,* many scenes if isolated would be revolting, but when considered in their context as the depiction of conflicts between virtues and vices—holiness and hypocrisy, temperance and gluttony, chastity and lust—they take on the aspect of ideal beauty. Likewise, in "Childe Roland to the Dark Tower Came," Browning, by picturing a repellant landscape and dwelling upon the ghastly reflections of Childe Roland, makes appear more beautiful the knight's indomitable courage in continuing his search when everything seems to counsel desistance. It is his feeling for beauty that gives the poet a sense of the right form in which to shape his thoughts; it gives him the right thoughts to shape. So high a place does it hold in the mind of poets that Keats said of it:

> Beauty is truth, truth beauty,—that is all
> Ye know on earth, and all ye need to know;

and W. B. Yeats added:

> The wrong of unshapely things is a wrong too great to be told.

Another characteristic is universality. The basic themes of poetry are love, death, and man's relation to his environment and to other men; and these are the common interests of all. But since the universal is best approached by way of the particular, poetry largely deals with individual experiences. These experiences, however, must be related to emotions which everyone feels, or the poem loses its validity. Hence such a poem as that by Robert Bridges which begins,

> I never shall love the snow again
> Since Maurice died,

although reflecting the author's personal loss, expresses as well the feeling of all who have suffered or might suffer similar loss. So inseparable is universality from poetry that a poem often will lay hold of a universal application without conscious will on the author's part. Thus Robert Frost in speaking of "Stopping by Woods on a Snowy Evening" once said that he wrote the poem without being conscious that it was more than a description of an isolated experience, but later he became aware that in the line,

> But I have promises to keep,

the poem had laid hold of so universal a matter as man's condition-ings, his duty to carry on the traditions of the race and fulfill promises made for him from the beginning of time. In similar way all good poetry deals with what is of universal import.

Another mark of poetry is sincerity. No writer who lacks honest conviction produces poetry of high merit. This is why those who grind out verse daily to meet some particular demand so rarely produce anything of value. Writing a poem a day may be good practice in skill for a beginner, but it is rare indeed that a poet, every single day of his existence, has a new idea upon which he feels deeply enough to write a poem. The poet who is sincere approaches his subject with freshness and vitality, even when his theme is old. Also the person who is writing merely to be clever rarely produces a poem of worth. Verse such as the following may divert and amuse, but it touches no deep emotion, nor does it give the intellectual satisfaction one demands of poetry.

(1)   Here lies the body of Solomon Pease,
      Under the daisies, under the trees,
      But Pease is not here, only the pod;
      Pease shelled out and went home to God.

(2)   Father's in the garden,
          Straining all his nerves;
      Mother's in the kitchen,
          Straining her preserves;
      Brother's straining muscles—
          But we can't rejoice,
      For sister's at the organ,
          Straining her poor voice.

(3)   Walking in a wood, a poet cried:
          "O Cuckoo, shall I call thee bird,
          Or but a wandering voice?"
      The school-examiner replied:
          "State the alternative preferred
          And reasons for the choice."

One has only to contrast these specimens with the following to catch the difference between amusing statements in rime and a sin-cere poem.

> She dwelt among the untrodden ways
>   Beside the springs of Dove,

[9]

A maid whom there were none to praise
And very few to love:

A violet by a mossy stone
Half hidden from the eye!
—Fair as a star, when only one
Is shining in the sky.

She lived unknown, and few could know
When Lucy ceased to be;
But she is in her grave, and, oh,
The difference to me!
—WILLIAM WORDSWORTH

It is not meant to imply here, of course, that humorous verse is likely to be uniformly of poor quality. Such verse may at times be employed to call attention to abuses or to ridicule absurdities, and it may have as sincere a purpose as the most serious poetry. Nor is it meant to imply that poems of the utmost sincerity may not be written on what appear to be slight themes. Such a poem, for instance, as Pope's "Rape of the Lock," at first seems to be much ado about a trifle, but a study of the poem discloses that Pope was doing more than writing about the theft of a lady's curl—that he was in reality making a serious criticism, in a mock heroic manner, of an artificial society. But if the theme is not important, the mood is; and the mood must always be sincere for the result to be entitled to the high name of poetry.

Another mark of poetry is restraint, the lack of which may lead to a false show of emotion and to the use of over-ornate language, both evidences of mediocrity. The power to place a proper check on feeling and on language, and from a simple situation to get the utmost expression, is always a mark of the supreme artist. An instance of this is in *Lear,* where Shakespeare has the old king, at last convinced of Cordelia's death, instead of bursting into a wild display of grief, look around dazedly, fumble at his collar, and say:

Pray you, undo this button: thank you, sir.

And another is in Webster's *Duchess of Malfi,* where the duchess, about to be slain at the instigation of her brothers, instead of break-ing into a passionate speech, says to her waiting woman:

I pray thee, look thou giv'st my little boy
Some syrup for his cold, and let the girl
Say her prayers ere she sleep.

Such restraint, exercised upon feelings powerfully surcharged with emotion, always induces a sense of strength and power, and aids in giving poetry its high effects.

Knowing some of the characteristics of a good poem is not enough, however, to give one a discriminating taste in poetry. Awareness of these characteristics will help, but this knowledge must be supplemented by much reading of poetry. To one not possessing the ability to distinguish an excellent poem from a mediocre one, a good way to make a start is to read in some good anthology until he finds a poem he likes, then turn to the verse in a newspaper that prints a "poem a day" by some author, and compare the two. If he does not at once discern the superiority of the former, repeat the process until he can. For a while, one not brought up from childhood to appreciate and understand the work of good poets must rely on the taste of more informed persons as to what is best. But if he will assume that the taste of men of fine training and high intelligence, especially if the opinions of such men coincide over a period of many generations, is likely to be more trustworthy than his own, limited as his must be by reason of inexperience, and if he will seek diligently to understand the poetry which they commend, he will come to recognize poetry from mere rime by its depth of thought and feeling, its heightened mood, its freshness even when dealing with old themes, its suggestiveness, its feeling for beauty, and its appeal to the imagination and the emotions.

It may be some time before he can appreciate such poems as *Paradise Lost* and *The Prelude;* but a failure to appreciate these is no disgrace at the beginning. If he is gradually acquiring more liking for poems which people with nice discrimination agree to be good, he may be satisfied. When, for instance, he prefers Longfellow to some writer of the "poem-a-day" type, he has made a start in the direction of poetic appreciation. When of Longfellow's poems he prefers "The Tide Rises, the Tide Falls" to "The Rainy Day" he has made more progress. When he prefers Shelley and Keats to Longfellow and Bryant, he has progressed further yet. And when he has an intelligent appreciation of such poems as Wordsworth's "I Wandered Lonely as a Cloud," Keats's "Ode on a Grecian Urn," Emerson's "Threnody," and Whitman's "Out of the Cradle Endlessly Rocking," he may be assured that he is on the way to knowing the best there is in poetry.

[11]

THE USES OF POETRY

All that has been said heretofore in this chapter has been to aid the student to recognize poetry and to help him arrive at the point where he will appreciate it. And now remains to give a few of the reasons why poetry is worth the best effort to understand it.

Perhaps the chief reason for knowing poetry is the intellectual delight it gives to a discriminating reader. The high thought, the lofty courage, the beautiful imagery of the poet, transmitted to us in words the most fitting for communication, arouse in us appropriate responses, and give us an aesthetic satisfaction which enriches life and gives us a greater capacity for its enjoyment.

But not only does poetry "serve for delight"; it benefits us in a number of practical ways. First, it acts in the manner of a catalytic agent, resolving our nebulous ideas and emotions, and producing new experiences. Thus since we live by experience, it enriches life for us, particularly as it leads us to understand and appreciate the outward beauty of the world as it is manifested in nature, and as it unfolds to us the working of the human spirit.

Furthermore, in a world where much sadness exists, the poet by writing of this in a beautiful way helps to heal our own sadness at this condition and enables us to bear the pains and losses which time brings.

Also, by startling us with vivid images, poetry quickens our sensibilities and makes us susceptible to suggestions that we ordinarily would pass by without note. And by associating dissimilar things and linking them by bold figures, it endears both to us—as, for instance, in Poe's lines "To Helen," where a woman's beauty and her classic features, the glory of Greece and the grandeur of Rome are brought together in such a way that our susceptibility to beauty is increased, while incidentally we come to have a more tender regard for the halcyon days of Greece and Rome.

And, to mention but one more use of poetry, by giving direc. tion and force to our thoughts, it leads us to action, so that what without it is only potential in us, becomes kinetic; and we, like the poet, in a sense become Makers.

This list might be extended much further, but no summary would be complete, for each will find many individual satisfactions in addition to those common to all lovers of poetry. If we read poetry day by day, our lives will inevitably become richer, and the way be increasingly clearer as to how we should think and, thinking, act.

CHAPTER III

THE LANGUAGE OF POETRY

ALL the effects which poetry secures it must secure through the medium of language. And since the effects which the poet attempts to build up result chiefly from an appeal to the emotions, and for that reason are fragile and hence likely to be destroyed by the slightest incongruity, the poet must select his words with the utmost discrimination. If he is dealing with ideas, he cannot risk explaining them with the same deliberation as the writer may whose appeal is chiefly to the reason, but must transmit them quickly and graphically so as to assure them the most favorable reception. If he is describing, he must give a clear and unblurred picture without undue dalliance lest he be charged with being prosaic and prolix. If he is expressing an emotion, he loses his effect unless he makes us feel the emotion acutely ourselves; and to do this requires the nicest choice of words, lest the emotion seem too sentimental on the one hand or too commonplace on the other. To such skill in the use of language, the poet has responded by evolving a style in which concrete terms predominate, figurative language is freely employed, and words are grouped according to special laws of language so as to produce the most pleasing sounds, or when the suggestions are not meant to be pleasing, the most accurate ones. In the following discussion of these aspects of the poetic style it is not meant to imply that they are peculiar to poetry alone. In some degree all these elements are present in prose, but there they are usually sporadic, while in poetry they are vital and indispensable.

CONCRETENESS
One of the characteristics of a poetic style is concreteness. Although chiefly interested in general and universal themes, the poet knows that the best way of stimulating interest in these is through the particular. He overcomes our lethargy and inattentiveness by forcing us to touch, taste, smell, hear, and see as he does. Through concrete terms he invokes vivid images, and by vivid images he transmits to us exact impressions, thus inducing in us something of his own clear vision.

This tendency to concreteness is evident in poetry in a number of ways, the most obvious being the employment of specific words and definite images to make tangible things which lack definite or exact dimensions or material qualities. Thus Tennyson refers to night as "the black bat"; Shakespeare speaks of "jocund day" standing "tip-toe on the misty mountain tops"; and Emily Dickinson thinks of twilight as "a dominie in gray." Further instances of the use of this method are the following descriptions by Shakespeare and Shelley, respectively, of winter and spring:

When icicles hang by the wall,
  And Dick the shepherd blows his nail,
And Tom bears logs into the hall,
  And milk comes frozen home in pail,
When blood is nipped, and ways be foul,
Then nightly sings the staring owl,
        Tu-whit;
Tu-who, a merry note,
While greasy Joan doth keel the pot.

When all aloud the wind doth blow,
  And coughing drowns the parson's saw,
And birds sit brooding in the snow,
  And Marian's nose looks red and raw,
When roasted crabs hiss in the bowl,
Then nightly sings the staring owl,
        Tu-whit;
Tu-who, a merry note,
While greasy Joan doth keel the pot.
                —*Love's Labour's Lost*, V, ii

Ah, woe is me! Winter is come and gone,
But grief returns with the revolving year;
The airs and streams renew their joyous tone;
The ants, the bees, the swallows reappear;
Fresh leaves and flowers deck the dead Seasons' bier;
The amorous birds now pair in every brake,
And build their mossy homes in field and brere;
And the green lizard, and the golden snake,
Like unimprisoned flames, out of their trance awake.
                —"Adonais"

Or again if the poet desires to describe an impersonal thing, he may vivify it by attributing to it personal characteristics, as Shelley does in "The Cloud":

I sift the snow on the mountains below,
And their great pines groan aghast;
And all the night 'tis my pillow white,
While I sleep in the arms of the blast.
Sublime on the towers of my skyey bowers,
Lightning my pilot sits;
In a cavern under is fettered the thunder,
It struggles and howls at fits.

Still another way in which the poet gains concreteness is by substituting actual figures for such abstractions as the soul, evil, good, virtue, truth, and honesty. This device, known as *allegory*, is frequently resorted to when the poet is dealing with abstract matters. Thus when Poe would describe insanity he does so in "The Haunted Palace" by representing a man's head as a palace once perfectly ordered but now filled with evil things. The most elaborate example of this in English poetry is Spenser's *Faerie Queene,* wherein the characters represent various virtues and vices. In more simple manner William Blake in "The Tiger" considers the creation of evil and the problem of its presence in the world by symbolizing it as a tiger. And Francis Thompson, thinking of the omnipresence of God's love and the inability of man to escape it, in "The Hound of Heaven" pictures God as a hound intent upon tracking down the errant soul, not to destroy, but to save it.

This tendency to employ concrete figures and specific words is apparent in the works of all the great poets. No page of Shakespeare is without examples. No one who dwelt so persistently as Shelley on general themes used more concrete terms than he. The poetaster may be content with glittering generalities, but the real poet makes us hear and touch and see.

FIGURATIVE LANGUAGE

Another characteristic of poetry is figurative language, which is but an added evidence of concreteness in poetry, for in the final analysis figures of speech are short cuts to the transmission of accurate ideas and exact images, conveying to us a definite impression of something with which we are likely to be unfamiliar, through a swift allusion or resemblance to an image already within our consciousness. Certain figurative forms—notably simile and metaphor, called figures of comparison; synecdoche and metonymy, called figures of association; and personification and apostrophe—are of so

[15]

frequent occurrence in poetry that the student should be acquainted with them.

A *comparison* likens two objects which belong to the same class, as when one says, "This hat is like yours." But when a direct comparison is made between objects that belong to different classes, the author is creating a figure called *simile*. Thus when Burns says "my luve is like a red, red rose," he compares love with a rose, and as *love* and *rose* belong to different classes, he has created a simile. A simile is usually introduced by *as* or *like*. A few more examples may be cited to illustrate its use:

> His legions—Angel Forms, who lay entranced
> Thick as autumnal leaves that strow the brooks
> In Vallombrosa, where the Etrurian shades
> High overarched embower; or scattered sedge
> Afloat, when with fierce winds Orion armed
> Hath vexed the Red-Sea coast.
> —MILTON, *Paradise Lost*, I

> Life, like a dome of many-colored glass,
> Stains the white radiance of eternity.
> —SHELLEY, "Adonais"

> Her hair that lay along her back
> Was yellow like ripe corn.
> —D. G. ROSSETTI, "The Blessed Damozel"

A *metaphor* is an implied comparison between objects of unlike classes. Instead of saying a thing *is like* another, it states that one thing *is* another. Thus when Longfellow speaks of a young girl as "a smile of God," and St. Paul says, "though I speak with the tongues of men and of angels," they imply a comparison but do not expressly state it, leaving the reader to register the various steps in his own mind. This is a bolder and more striking figure than the simile, and is used frequently in poetry. Other examples are:

> Awake! for Morning in the Bowl of Night
> Has flung the stone that puts the stars to flight:
> And lo! the Hunter of the East has caught
> The Sultán's Turret in a noose of Light.
> —FITZGERALD, *The Rubáiyát*

> Death, thou'rt a cordial old and rare:
> Look how compounded, with what care!

Time got his wrinkles reaping thee
Sweet herbs from all antiquity.
—LANIER, "The Stirrup-Cup"

Sometimes whole poems are sustained metaphors, examples being Tennyson's "Crossing the Bar," Whitman's "O Captain! My Captain!" and Francis Thompson's "The Hound of Heaven." An allegory, also, has the qualities of a sustained metaphor, since it is the representation by means of a figurative story of something different which is suggested but not stated.

Another form of comparison is *analogy,* defined in Webster's *New International Dictionary* as "A relation of likeness, *between* two things or *of* one thing *to* or *with* another, consisting in the resemblance not of the things themselves but of two or more attributes, circumstances, or effects; thus, the *analogy* between sleep and death lies in the attendant cessation of activity and appearance of repose. . . ."

Metonymy is the describing of an object by naming something closely associated with it, as when we say, "He keeps a good table" instead of "good food"; or "Our ships opened fire" instead of "our sailors"; or as in the line from "A Dream of Fair Women," where instead of saying, "the knife quivered," Tennyson says, "The bright death quivered at the victim's throat."

Synecdoche is the using of a part for the whole, the whole for a part, the genus for the species, or the species for the genus, as in such examples as "Fifty winters passed him by" instead of "fifty years"; and "the halcyon year" for "summer." In modern usage metonymy and synecdoche are infrequently distinguished, the former term being used loosely for either.

Personification is attributing to abstract or inanimate objects qualities of life, as in the following:

Stern Daughter of the Voice of God!
O Duty! if that name thou love
Who art a light to guide, a rod
To check the erring and reprove.
—WORDSWORTH, "Ode to Duty"

Swiftly walk o'er the western wave,
Spirit of Night!
Out of the misty eastern cave,
Where, all the long and lone daylight,

[17]

Thou wovest dreams of joy and fear
Which make thee terrible and dear,—
Swift be thy flight!
—SHELLEY, "To Night"

Apostrophe is addressing an inanimate object as if alive, or addressing directly as if present one absent or dead, as in such examples as the following:

Ye flowery banks o' bonnie Doon,
How can ye blume sae fair!
—BURNS, "The Banks o' Doon"

Milton! thou shouldst be living at this hour.
—WORDSWORTH, "Sonnet to Milton"

Ah what avails the sceptred race!
Ah what the form divine!
What every virtue, every grace!
Rose Aylmer, all were thine.
—LANDOR, "Rose Aylmer"

ALLUSIONS

Another characteristic of poetry, not so common as concreteness or figurative language, but in considerable evidence nevertheless, is the reference to other literature or to historical events. Such references are called *allusions*. The most important storehouses of literature which poets ransack for images, ideas, and suggestions as a means of enriching their own work and insuring certain connotations in their verse are the classic myths, the Bible, and for those of later times the older poets, particularly Shakespeare. To catch the significance of such references it is necessary to have acquaintance with the poet's source; and as our knowledge of these sources increases, our enjoyment of poetry will tend to become greater, since our interest in the matter we are reading is enhanced by associating with it ideas we have come upon elsewhere. Some examples of allusions, arranged roughly in the order of their difficulty, follow:

The sparrows chirped as if they still were proud
Their race in Holy Writ should mentioned be;
And hungry crows, assembled in a crowd,
Clamored their piteous prayer incessantly,
Knowing who hears the ravens cry, and said:
"Give us, O Lord, this day our daily bread!"

.   .   .   .   .

And thrifty farmers, as they tilled the earth,
  Heard with alarm the cawing of the crow,
That mingled with the universal mirth,
  Cassandra-like, prognosticating woe.
          —LONGFELLOW, "The Birds of Killingworth"

Minerva, the inventress of the flute,
Flung it aside, when she her face surveyed
Distorted in a fountain as she played;
The unlucky Marsyas found it, and his fate
Was one to make the bravest hesitate.
          —LONGFELLOW, "Morituri Salutamus"

  The healing of His seamless dress
    Is by our beds of pain;
  We touch Him in life's throng and press,
    And we are whole again.
          —WHITTIER, "Our Master"

  Of Deborah who mustered
    Her brethren long oppressed,
  And routed the heathen army,
    And gave her people rest.
          —BRYANT, "A Lifetime"

  I know what say the fathers wise,—
  The book itself before me lies,
  Old *Chrysostom*, best Augustine,
  And he who blent both in his line,
  The younger *Golden Lips* or mines,
  Taylor, the Shakespeare of divines.
          —EMERSON, "The Problem"

  Heroes are much the same, the point's agreed,
  From Macedonia's madman to the Swede.
          —POPE, "Essay on Man"

The loon, that seemed to mock some goblin tryst,
Laughed; and the echoes, huddling in affright,
Like Odin's hounds, fled baying down the night.
    —J. R. LOWELL, "The Washers of the Shroud"

  I held it truth, with him who sings
    To one clear harp in divers tones,
    That men may rise on stepping-stones
  Of their dead selves to higher things.
          —TENNYSON, "In Memoriam"

Oh, could you take them by surprise,
You'd find Schidone's eager Duke
Doing the quaintest courtesies
To that prim saint by Haste-thee-Luke!
And, deeper into her rock den,
Bold Castelfranco's Magdalen
You'd find retreated from the ken
Of that robed counsel-keeping Ser—
As if the Tizian thinks of her.
     —BROWNING, "In a Gondola"

SPECIAL DEVICES

In addition to concrete and figurative language, poetry has a somewhat greater tendency than prose to make use of certain special devices of style, two of which are worth noting. One of these, *sentence inversion,* although frowned upon by contemporary poets, was formerly used frequently to secure emphasis or to make riming easier or to make the words fit more readily into the metrical scheme. An instance of the use of inversion to gain emphasis for certain parts of a sentence is the following:

Him the Almighty Power
Hurled headlong flaming from the ethereal sky,
With hideous ruin and combustion, down
To bottomless perdition.
     —MILTON, *Paradise Lost,* I

Another device, *antithesis* or *the balanced sentence,* is used for the purpose of emphasis or to give a greater vivacity to the ideas by contrasting or comparing them. This device, a favorite of Elizabethan writers, reached the peak of its popularity in the eighteenth century. These lines from Pope illustrate its effective use:

Be not the first by whom the new are try'd,
Nor yet the last to lay the old aside.
     —*Essay on Criticism*

'Tis education forms the common mind.
Just as the twig is bent, the tree's inclin'd.
Boastful and rough, your first son is a squire;
The next a tradesman, meek, and much a liar;
Tom struts a soldier, open, bold, and brave;
Will sneaks a scriv'ner, an exceeding knave.
     —*Moral Essays,* I

TONE QUALITY

In addition to the more objective elements already discussed in this chapter, others exist, more subjective in quality, which are also vital parts of the poetic style. These relate largely to the grouping of words so as to produce pleasing or accurate sounds, and depend on vowel and consonant relationships or on an imaginative suggestiveness. Their main function is to produce melody and harmony, but they serve also to emphasize certain elements of verse, and thus have a double utility.

First may be considered the quality of certain sounds. A student will not progress far in the analysis of verse before discovering that poets take every available opportunity of assimilating sound to sense by a careful selection of vowels and consonants which aid in producing the effects the sense requires. Thus they make use of long vowels to suggest slow and deliberate movement and of short ones to suggest hurry. Note in the following examples, for instance, how in the first, long vowels aid in retarding the movement of the lines, thus helping to suggest the proper atmosphere of the poem, while in the second, the vowels force one to read quickly, thus again suggesting the proper atmosphere.[1]

> The curfew tolls the knell of parting day,
>   The lowing herd winds slowly o'er the lea,
> The ploughman homeward plods his weary way,
>   And leaves the world to darkness and to me.
>   —GRAY, "Elegy in a Country Churchyard"

> I come from haunts of coot and hern,
>   I make a sudden sally
> And sparkle out among the fern,
>   To bicker down a valley.
>   —TENNYSON, "The Brook"

Of the consonants, the *liquids, l, m, n, r,* combine easily with other sounds and are used frequently where the verse is to be read rapidly. Note how many liquids Lanier employs in the following lines from "The Song of the Chattahoochee" in an effort to suggest the rush of water downhill:

> I hu*rr*y a*main* to *r*each the p*l*ai*n*,
>   *R*un the *r*apid a*n*d *l*eap the fa*ll*,
> Sp*l*it at the *r*ock a*n*d togethe*r* agai*n*.

[1] The student should not assume that the whole effect gained here is through the choice of vowels. Various other elements, discussed elsewhere, enter. The point to observe now is that the long and short vowels *aid* in giving the effect desired. This same caution should be borne in mind in what is said hereafter of consonants.

On the other hand, a group of consonants, called *mutes,* are the most difficult of all to utter, because they close the air passages, and hence are used to suggest impediments and to force a slower movement of the verse. There are three groups of these: *labials* (lip sounds), *b, f, p, v; dentals* (tooth sounds), *d, t, dh, th;* and *gutturals* (throat sounds), hard *c, g,* and *k.* In Lanier's poem just mentioned, for instance, after suggesting by the use of liquids the rush of the stream, he employs mutes to suggest the hindrances imposed on it, and, by slowing the reading of the lines, actually indicates the impediments in the way of the water's rush:

> All down the hills of Habersham,
>   All through the valleys of Hall,
> The rushes cried *Abide, abide,*
> The willful waterweeds held me thrall,
> The laving laurel turned my tide,
> The ferns and the fondling grass said *Stay,*
> The dewberry dipped for to work delay,
> And the little reeds sighed *Abide, abide,*
>   *Here in the hills of Habersham,*
>   *Here in the valleys of Hall.*
>
> High o'er the hills of Habersham,
>   Veiling the valleys of Hall,
> The hickory told me manifold
> Fair tales of shade; the poplar tall
> Wrought me her shadowy self to hold;
> The chestnut, the oak, the walnut, the pine,
> Overleaning, with flickering meaning and sign,
> Said, *Pass not, so cold, these manifold*
>   *Deep shades of the hills of Habersham,*
>   *These glades in the valleys of Hall.*

Still another group of consonants, the *sibilants, s, z, sh,* and *zh,* which make hissing sounds or are spoken in a whisper, are used to gain such effects as surprise, solicitude, amazement, and contempt.

In addition to the use of vowels and consonants already described, some special uses occur, the chief purpose of which is to emphasize certain sounds. These are alliteration, assonance, consonance, and onomatopœia.

Alliteration is the repetition of initial letters or sounds in neighboring words, as in the following:

Five miles meandering with a mazy motion.
    —COLERIDGE, "Kubla Khan"

It was the season, when through all the land
    The merle and mavis build, and building sing
Those lovely lyrics, written by His hand,
    Whom Saxon Cædmon calls the blithe-heart King.
        —LONGFELLOW, "The Birds of Killingworth"

Assonance is the agreement of vowel sounds in words wherein the consonant sounds differ, as in the phrase "Molten golden notes." It is usually employed as supplementary to rime as an emphasiz-ing element, but in the following poem replaces rime:

Maiden, crowned with glossy blackness,
    Lithe as panther forest-roaming,
Long-armed naiad, when she dances,
    On a stream of ether floating,—
    Bright, O bright Fedalma!

Form all curves like softness drifted,
    Wave-kissed marble roundly dimpling,
Far-off music slowly winged,
    Gently rising, gently sinking,—
    Bright, O bright Fedalma!
        —GEORGE ELIOT, *The Spanish Gypsy*, I

In *Hiawatha,* which also lacks rime, Longfellow employs assonance constantly.

Consonance is an agreement of final consonant sounds when the vowel sounds differ, as mi*le,* ti*ll,* or as in the lines:

Proud and unafraid he stood,
Nor said a word to those around.

Like assonance, it is usually supplementary to rime, and is employed less frequently than alliteration and assonance.

Onomatopœia is the use of words in which the sound suggests the sense, as in *buzz, hiss, clang, splash, murmur,* and the like. Such words, chosen for their imaginative suggestiveness, are fre-quent in poetry. Note, for instance, the effective use of this de-vice in the following examples:

The moan of doves in immemorial elms,
And murmuring of innumerable bees.
        —TENNYSON, *The Princess,* VII

All day within the dreamy house,
The doors upon their hinges creak'd;
The blue fly sung in the pane; the mouse
Behind the mouldering wainscot shriek'd.
—TENNYSON, "Mariana"

A tap at the pane, the quick sharp scratch
And blue spurt of a lighted match.
—BROWNING, "Meeting at Night"

More sustained examples are Poe's "Bells," Browning's "How They Brought the Good News from Ghent to Aix," and Vachel Lindsay's "Sante-Fé Trail."

RIME

The most effective grouping of vowels and consonants to give pleasing results is that which produces rime. As employed in English poetry, rime is the correspondence, in two or more words, of terminal sounds—that is, of the last accented vowel and the sounds following it, if there are any, but with different sounds preceding the accented vowel. Thus *pose, rose,* and *close* rime, but not *pose* and *suppose* (because the consonant sounds preceding the accented vowel *o* are similar),[2] nor *rose* and *host* (because the sounds after the accented vowels differ). Rime, then, is a matter of sound, not of spelling; hence *high* and *buy* rime, but not *now* and *snow*.

Rime is called *single* or *masculine* when only single syllables rime (e.g., all, pall), *double* or *feminine* when two syllables rime (e.g., raven, craven), and *triple* when three syllables rime (e.g., violet, triolet).

The usual position of rimed words is at the end of lines. This is called *end rime*. But not infrequently words that rime are found within the line. This is called *internal rime*. The following examples illustrate internal as well as end rime:

Once upon a midnight *dreary*, while I pondered weak and *weary*,
Over many a quaint and curious volume of forgotten lore—
While I nodded, nearly *napping*, suddenly there came a *tapping*,

[2] In French poetry and in early English poetry words of similar sound rime, particularly if they have different meanings, as in Chaucer's lines:

The holy blisful martir for to seke,
That hem hath holpen, whan that they were seke;

but modern English poets avoid this usage.

As of some one gently *rapping, rapping* at my chamber door.
" 'Tis some visitor," I muttered, *"tapping* at my chamber door—
Only this, and nothing more."
—Poe, "The Raven"

The splendor *falls* on castle *walls*
And snowy summits old in story;
The long light *shakes* across the *lakes,*
And the wild cataract leaps in glory.
—Tennyson, *The Princess,* IV

The function of rime.—Rime has three principal functions. First, it serves as a melodic element, the recurrence of similar sounds at regular intervals enhancing the tone quality and adding to the pleasurable emotions awakened by reading poetry, particularly reading it, or hearing it read, aloud. Second, it serves to emphasize the riming words, thus bringing them into prominence in the verse. For example, in "The Raven" Poe, by a skilful repetition in stanza after stanza of words ending with the sound ōre, places a constantly growing emphasis on these words and consequently on the ideas they present. Another sort of emphasis is illustrated by a stanza from Shelley's "To a Skylark":

Sound of vernal showers
On the twinkling grass,
Rain-awakened flowers,
All that ever was
Joyous, and clear, and fresh, thy music doth surpass.

Here the verb *was,* which ordinarily is glided over, is made to assume a high importance in the stanza because it is one of the riming words and is forced to bear an accent. Third, rime serves as an organizing agent in the grouping of lines into stanzas, but since this is perhaps its most important function, its use in this respect will be taken up at greater length in the chapter dealing with the stanza.

CHAPTER IV

ON STUDYING THE CONTENT OF POETRY

IN describing a man, we usually give a separate account of his appearance and of his character, first noting his build and features, and then passing to a relation of his opinions, attitudes, ideas, and philosophy. Yet in considering him in our mind, we hardly think of his physique and his innate qualities—intellectual or spiritual—as separate entities, but of all as combining to make a complete being. This is but an analogy of the way in which we customarily approach the study of a poem. The poem is a synthesis of form and content, which in the last analysis are inseparable. Yet just as we commonly describe a man's appearance apart from his innate qualities, we find it more convenient to study separately the content and the structure of a poem, as if each existed independently of the other.

Of the two—form and content—the latter is almost always the more important, for it is the idea of a poem that interests us primarily; and a knowledge of the language and structure is but a help to a more complete comprehension of the content. Since this is true, we shall first consider how to study the content of a poem, and in later chapters give attention to its form and structure.

DISCOVERING THE PURPOSE OF A POEM

A poem does one of four things: it tells a story; it presents a picture; it expresses an emotional experience; or it reflects on life. Often it does two or more of these, but even when this is true, one purpose is usually dominant. A first step, therefore, is to determine which the poet is trying to do in any given poem. This is usually not difficult, particularly if the poem tells a story or presents a picture of a scene or person. Even when the poem gives expression to an emotion or is a reflection on some phase of existence, the student after a little practice should be able to tell for what purpose the author wrote it. And then having done this, he is ready to begin a more careful study of it.

If the poem tells a story, the student should of course know the details of the narrative. He should also form as clear a picture as possible of those participating in the action. And then he should try to find the reason for the poet's telling the story. Was it merely to please or entertain, as was Holmes's purpose in "The Deacon's Masterpiece," Lowell's in "The Courtin'," and Alfred Noyes's in "The Highwayman"? Was it to teach a lesson of some sort, as in "The Rime of the Ancient Mariner," where aside from other considerations Coleridge attempts to show that

> He prayeth best, who loveth best
> All things both great and small;

or as in "Rhœcus," where Lowell tries to show that

> . . . he who scorns the least of Nature's works
> Is thenceforth exiled and shut out from all?

Or was it to arouse in us a sense of pity, sympathy, fear, patriotism, or the like, as in "The Building of the Ship," by Longfellow, or "The Snare," by James Stephens?

If the poem presents a picture of a scene or a person, the student should try to see what the poet is describing as nearly as possible as he saw it. Then he should try to determine the author's reason for presenting the picture. He should be warned, however, against trying to find some deep purpose in every poem of this sort, for not uncommonly a poet may see a place, be pleased or surprised or repelled by its beauty or ugliness or some other circumstance about it, and write a poem merely to express his feeling at the time. Such a poem is Wordsworth's sonnet, "Composed upon Westminster Bridge":

> Earth has not anything to show more fair:
> Dull would he be of soul who could pass by
> A sight so touching in its majesty:
> This city now doth, like a garment, wear
> The beauty of the morning; silent, bare,
> Ships, towers, domes, theatres, and temples lie
> Open unto the fields, and to the sky;
> All bright and glittering in the smokeless air.
> Never did sun more beautifully steep
> In his first splendor, valley, rock, or hill;
> Ne'er saw I, never felt, a calm so deep!
> The river glideth at his own sweet will:
> Dear God! the very houses seem asleep;
> And all that mighty heart is lying still!

If the purpose of the poem is to express an emotional experience, it is necessary to perceive what was the emotion which the poet felt and, for a complete comprehension of the poem, to be able to tell what evoked the emotion. Often, in addition to this, something of the character of the author can be adduced from the poem. An example of this type of poem in which it is possible to tell all these things is Christina Rossetti's "A Birthday":

> My heart is like a singing bird
>   Whose nest is in a watered shoot;
> My heart is like an apple-tree
>   Whose boughs are bent with thickset fruit;
> My heart is like a rainbow shell
>   That paddles in a halcyon sea;
> My heart is gladder than all these
>   Because my love is come to me.
>
> Raise me a dais of silk and down;
>   Hang it with vair and purple dyes;
> Carve it in doves and pomegranates,
>   And peacocks with a hundred eyes;
> Work it in gold and silver grapes,
>   In leaves and silver fleurs-de-lys;
> Because the birthday of my life
>   Is come, my love is come to me.

If the poem is one which reflects on life, either broadly or in some restricted way, it is essential to understand the attitude of the author, to try to discover his basic philosophy, and to know something of the matter he is considering, so as to evaluate intelligently his contribution and judge his worth. Since poets are supremely interested in human happiness and in the relation of man to man and of man to his universe, a large number of poems belong to this group; and even when his chief interest is in telling a story, expressing some personal feeling, or depicting a scene, the poet will often incorporate incidental reflections on life. When this latter is done, the student should be able to determine whether the reflection is incidental, and distinguish poems containing merely incidental reflections from those designed primarily to comment upon some phase of existence.

READING A POEM

Although the end of the study of poetry is not merely to learn to read it intelligently, the knowledge of how to read it must precede any understanding of it or liking for it, for out of thoughtful reading comes understanding; and out of understanding, apprecia· tion; and out of appreciation, a new approach to thinking—in fine, a new life itself. Since, then, a failure to apprehend poetry is usually the result of inability to read it intelligently, one of the first steps necessary to its understanding is to acquire a few simple principles of reading.

Because poetry differs from prose in some of its qualities, many who can read prose intelligently make but a poor attempt at understanding poetry. One of these differences is the arrangement of matter on the page. Poetry is arranged according to a metrical scheme which frequently does not coincide with rhetorical divisions. Yet many persons read verse according to the metrical arrangement, pausing at the end of each line, whether a natural pause comes there or not, and in general paying little attention to the rhetorical divisions. One of the first things to realize in reading poetry is that the rules of punctuation apply here just as in prose, and that the arrangement by lines has to do with metrical, not rhetorical, requirements. No one reads prose a line at a time, rushing over all the devices which mark pauses, and pausing arbitrarily at the end of each line; yet that is the manner in which many people try to read poetry. It is little wonder, therefore, that they fail to understand what they are reading. If the student will read with regard to normal rhetorical pauses, the metre and melody will take care of themselves.

Another difference is in the order of words. Modern poetry, it is true, tends to follow the normal word order found in prose, but this is not so true of the older poetry. The student, therefore, must take note of inversions and the transposition of sentence elements, and of elisions. It may be well enough to learn to read the daily newspaper or popular fiction by glancing rapidly over whole paragraphs at a time, but poetry, no more than an advanced work on science, can be read thus. The way to read poetry is word by word, aloud if possible, so as to miss nothing of the "flavor" of the words, and with an understanding of the relationship between them.

But not only does poetry differ from prose in sentence structure and the arrangement on the page; the poet in general refers more fleetingly to his emotional experiences and condenses ideas more than does the novelist or the essayist. Often there is no introduction, and but little effort to orientate a reader to a situation. The poet starts *in medias res,* and after expressing the quintessence of his idea or emotion, stops. It is left to the reader to supply the gaps, to build up and complete the picture. The poet also as a rule is more subtle than is the writer of prose: he connotes, implies, rather than elucidates at length. There are usually clues, to be sure, but they are not dwelt upon as the writer of prose dwells on them; instead, they are insinuated so casually into the poem that they are likely to escape the attention of a careless reader.

Not infrequently, answering a few very elementary questions will set a student on the right track and lead to a correct interpretation of a poem. Such questions as the following, for instance, are not too elementary to start with, and if the student is inclined to consider them too simple for anyone past childhood, he might experiment by trying them on, say, Browning's "My Last Duchess" and "Fra Lippo Lippi" and E. A. Robinson's "Partnership."

First, who is speaking in the poem—the poet himself or some character he has created? And if the latter, what is the character of the speaker? Is it a man or a woman? Is he illiterate or educated? What is his mood at the time he is speaking?

Second, to whom is the person speaking? To any chance reader, to a particular type of reader, or to some particular person described or suggested in the poem itself? If it is the latter, what is the relation of the listener to the speaker? What is the attitude of each? And what can be told of their character from what is said?

Third, what is the setting of the poem: a seaside? a mountainside? a picture gallery? a drawing room? How is the action, dialogue, or situation conditioned by the setting? Obviously no setting is necessary in many types of poetry, but occasionally to get a clear idea of the setting is to come to a clearer understanding of the poem itself.

Fourth, in what age, season, month, or even at what time of day does a poem take place? Again such answers are not possible for all poems. A poem which expresses feeling primarily, for instance, or which reflects on life in some general way may be timeless; but in many poems an understanding of the time when the words of a poem are spoken helps greatly to illuminate the poem.

Fifth, what suggested the poem, or what particular emotion or situation evoked it? This is often a difficult question for one just beginning the study of poetry, but when it can be answered, it will usually lead to a full understanding of the poem.

Sixth, what is the poet's intention. Is it merely to entertain or please, or does he seek to arouse in some way the emotion of his readers, or is he trying to teach some lesson? If he is trying to arouse an emotion, what particular emotion does he seek to awaken: pity, fear, sympathy, or some other?

Besides the questions suggested, which apply to individual poems, there are others to ask when studying the work of a single poet, such for instance as these: What aspects of life interest the author? Is his chief preoccupation with nature or humanity? If the former, is it with landscapes, seascapes, such larger segments as mountains, prairies, valleys, or with such things as birds and bees and flowers? If his chief interest is humanity, is he interested in the whole of the race, with certain types, or with individuals, and in what way? Is he interested in normal or abnormal qualities in people? Or is he interested in art and beauty for their own sake, apart from their influence on human development? What is the dominant attitude and feeling in all his work? Has he an optimistic or pessimistic view of life? Is he a mystic, an agnostic, or an atheist? Is he concerned chiefly with himself or with others: is he an extrovert or introvert? Is he interested primarily in love, death, religion, patriotism, social relationships, and in what particular aspects of these? To ask and answer such questions as these will not "spoil poetry" for one, but will lead to the most complete understanding, and thence to the highest appreciation, of a poet's work.

Finally, whether he is interpreting a single poem or all the work of a poet, the student's aim should be that which is supposed to animate a witness in court: to tell the truth, the whole truth, and nothing but the truth— that is, to get all the author meant to convey, but avoid reading into the poem meanings which the author never intended. Such an aim cannot be attained at once by a student whose training in reading poetry is meager. To give the general sense of a poem is possible before one progresses far in the study of poetry, but to get all the connotations and suggestions is harder, and to avoid reading into a poem what the author never intended to be there is hardest of all. Intellectual inertia, indifference, and lack of sensitivity on the part of the student, as well as the belief that analysis will spoil a poem for one, prevents his seeing all the author meant; while the belief, usually grounded in early training at the hands of incompetent teachers, that there is something mysterious about poetry which prevents any save advanced students from understanding it, or a romantic disposition to outrun the imagination of the poet, often leads to a symbolical or allegorical interpretation when a literal one will suffice. The safe method is to analyze a poem stanza by stanza, interpreting it literally so long as such an interpretation will suffice, and accepting symbolism or allegory only when the poet's clues to such an interpretation are unmistakable, or when a literal interpretation fails to offer a satisfactory explanation. Such a basis does not, of course, prohibit one from receiving from a poem suggestions and ideas which the author may not have had in mind, but it prevents him from confusing his own reactions with the ideas of the poet.

CHAPTER V

THE MAIN CLASSES OF POETRY

ALTHOUGH poetry may be classified in a number of ways, the most common classification is by types. In this classification the point of view of the author and his method of composition determine the category to which the poem belongs. Classified thus, poetry is narrative, lyric, or dramatic.[1]

THE THREE TYPES DISTINGUISHED

If the author tells a story, if he stands, as it were, on the sidelines and sets down his observations as a reporter does, if his presentation is largely objective, the poem belongs to the category of narrative poetry. If on the other hand the poetry is subjective, if it is concerned chiefly with the author's personal emotions, moods, feelings, ideas, and reflections, if it is biased by his idiosyncrasies and philosophy, the poem belongs to the category of lyric poetry. And if the author combines these two forms, telling the story so far as he is concerned objectively, but embodying the emotional experiences of the characters and relating the story in their words by means of dialogue, it belongs to the category of dramatic poetry.

SUBDIVISIONS OF NARRATIVE POETRY

Subdivisions of narrative poetry are the heroic epic, the literary epic, the mock epic, the metrical romance, the popular ballad, the literary ballad, and the metrical tale.

The term *epic* is from the Greek ἔπος, a story, and ἐπικός, pertaining to a story, and designates the highest and most elaborate form of narrative poetry. The *heroic epic* relates a great struggle, conflict, or movement of a whole people or nation, and represents national ideals and preoccupations. There is usually a central figure, about whom the action revolves, who is endowed with supernatural qualities, and who symbolizes racial or national predilec-

---

[1] Other classifications are (1) according to the treatment of the themes, as realistic, romantic, etc.; (2) according to its chief interest, as nature, love, death, religion, patriotism, etc.; and (3) according to structure, as blank verse, free verse, and stanzaic forms.

tions and aspirations. Examples of the heroic epic are the *Iliad,* the *Odyssey, Beowulf,* and the *Nibelungenlied.* Such poems doubt-less began as communal efforts, were passed on by word of mouth from generation to generation, gaining accretions in this progress, gradually took on definite shape, and finally became crystallized as the poems we know.[2]

The *literary epic* resembles the heroic epic in that it is written in a high and lofty vein and deals with tribal, national, or racial movements and struggles; and is different in that it is the product of a poet who in a literary age attempts to produce a poem in the manner of the heroic epic. Outstanding examples of the literary epic are Virgil's *Aeneid,* Tasso's *Jerusalem Delivered,* and Milton's *Paradise Lost.*

The *mock epic* is a poem which employs the grandiloquent language and the elaborate machinery of the heroic epic while dealing with a theme of trifling significance. Its purpose is usually ridicule, although it may be used in a whimsical way to give mock significance to some trifle. Examples are Samuel Butler's *Hudibras* and Joel Barlow's *Hasty Pudding.*

The *metrical romance* is a long tale of love and adventure which attained high popularity in the Middle Ages. It is remi-niscent of the epic in some ways, but deals not so much with a national struggle or racial traits as with the wonderful adventures of a central figure, endowed with superhuman abilities, and the sur-prising incidents growing out of some quest on which he embarks. The medieval tales about King Arthur and Amadis of Gaul belong to this *genre,* as does Spenser's *Faerie Queene.*

The *popular ballad* is a folk product. In old days when there were no newspapers, and when the common folk had no books or, in still earlier times, no manuscripts, happenings which today would be news stories were made into songs and passed along by word of mouth. Doubtless some of these stories were composed entirely by one person, but often they were a synthesis of the efforts of sev-eral persons, each adding a stanza or so as his contribution to the theme. Even if a ballad was the work of one author, the identity of the composer was soon lost, and the ballad became community property, was passed along by word of mouth, often becoming cor-rupt in the process and occasionally gathering new stanzas as it

[2] Whether in their final form they were shaped and unified by one man, as the *Iliad* and the *Odyssey* by Homer, is a question on which scholars differ, and which we need not here try to resolve.

went along, until at last it was written down by some collector and preserved in the archives of literature. Thus the ballad resembles the heroic epic in origin but differs from it in almost all other respects. The epic deals with high, heroic themes, the ballad with those common to ordinary people; the epic treats of racial or national activities, the ballad of personal deeds, frequently of single episodes, although at times a number of single episodes relating to one person are strung together in a story, as in the Robin Hood ballads of England or the Jesse James ballads of our own West. Qualities of the ballad are its simplicity of theme and form; its impersonal tone through the expression of community rather than personal feeling; its tendency towards melodrama; its lack of rhetorical devices save simple rime, repetition, and refrain; the restriction of its interests to the elementary emotions, such as love, hate, jealousy, fear, and cupidity; and its preoccupation with subjects of folk interest. Its themes are domestic and love tragedies; folk lore and superstition; border and civil warfare; outlawry; humor, usually of a broad or farcical sort; greenwood—or in our time hobo—life; and those relating to the occupations of certain classes, as weavers, cowboys, stevedores, and lumbermen. Examples are "Barbara Allan," "The Wife of Usher's Well," "Chevy Chase," "Robin Hood and Guy of Gisborne," and "Jesse James."

The *literary ballad* resembles the popular ballad in theme and treatment but, instead of being a communal product, it is the work of one poet who is consciously imitating the popular ballad. The range is from such close imitations as Chatterton's "Dethe of Syr Charles Bawdin," Scott's "Proud Maisie," and Allan Cunningham's "Young Maxwell" to such purely literary pieces as Coleridge's "Rime of the Ancient Mariner" and Keats's "La Belle Dame sans Merci." Other examples are Longfellow's "Wreck of the Hesperus," Robert Bridges' "Screaming Tarn," and Badger Clark's "Glory Trail."

Besides these formal divisions of narrative poetry there is a further division in which for convenience may be placed a great many poems that are episodical in character, are told objectively, and yet are lacking in the precise qualities of the epic, romance, or ballad. These range from long historical narratives, such as Scott's *Marmion* and Alfred Noyes's *Drake,* to such short ones as Macaulay's "Horatius," Holmes's "Grandmother's Story of Bunker-Hill Battle," and Longfellow's "Paul Revere's Ride"; and from long metrical tales, like Longfellow's *Evangeline* and Tennyson's *Enoch*

[35]

Arden, to such brief episodes as Joaquin Miller's "Kit Carson's Ride" and Lowell's "Rhœcus." Such poems are called *metrical tales,* or sometimes simply *stories in verse.*

SUBDIVISIONS OF LYRIC POETRY

Since the body of lyric poetry is so large and the types grouped under this term so diverse, a more arbitrary method of subdividing has to be employed than with narrative poetry. One method is to group the poems according to theme, as lyrics of love, nature, death (elegiac poetry), religion, patriotism, and the like. Such a method is satisfactory, but it needs no extended comment, since poems dealing with these various themes are easily distinguished. Frequently, however, when such division is made, the sonnet, the ode, reflective poetry, didactic poetry, and satirical poetry are treated as if coordinate with these groups. And here we meet with difficulties, for although virtually all sonnets are lyrics, the sonnet has to do primarily with form, and there is no absolute reason why it might not tell a story, while Shakespeare actually uses it in the dialogue parts of some of his dramas. Certainly a sonnet might be a nature or love poem, and an ode might be didactic, and a poem about nature might be incidentally a satire. Hence to avoid this confusion, although the arrangement is not an ideal one because no sharp line can be drawn between the groups which follow, it seems best here to base the subdivisions on the intensity of the lyric expression, and to treat such forms as the sonnet, the ode, the villanelle, and the like, in a separate division, which deals with the structure of poems.

The song.—Although the original meaning of lyric—a poem composed to be sung to the accompaniment of the lyre—is now discarded in favor of a definition that will admit the whole range of subjective poetry, songs comprise a large section of modern lyric poetry. There are two classes of these, secular and sacred; and they range from airy trifles to deeply serious and reflective hymns of worship. The themes are as various as the moods of mankind, but the most common subjects for secular songs are love, nature, and patriotism; and of sacred songs, religion, death, and immortality. Good examples of the former are John Lyly's "Apelles' Song," Shakespeare's "Who Is Sylvia," "O Mistress Mine," and "Fear No More the Heat o' th' Sun," Ben Jonson's "Drink to Me Only with Thine Eyes," Thomas Campion's "Cherry-Ripe," Burns's "Auld Lang Syne" and "Banks o' Doon," Thomas Moore's " 'Tis the Last Rose of Summer," and the songs of Stephen Foster; and of the latter, Isaac Watts's "Our God, Our Help in Ages Past," Charles Wesley's "Jesus, Lover of My Soul," Cardinal Newman's "Lead, Kindly Light," O. W. Holmes's "Hymn of Trust," Whittier's "Eternal Goodness," and Kipling's "God of Our Fathers."

The pure lyric.—Next are poems which because of their highly personal and emotional qualities, their simple structure, and their brevity may be designated as pure lyrics. In general they are brief and have simple rime-schemes, permitting them to be set to music; they treat but a single emotion and are superior in literary quality to most songs. Some of the best examples of this group are Herrick's "To Daffodils," Waller's "Go, Lovely Rose," Wordsworth's "A Slumber Did My Spirit Seal," "I Wandered Lonely as a Cloud," and "Solitary Reaper," Byron's "She Walks in Beauty" and "So We'll Go No More a-Roving," Shelley's "To Night," Landor's "Rose Aylmer," Poe's "To Helen," and Lanier's "Evening Song."

The longer lyric.—A further group is differentiated from that just considered by its sustained emotion and its elaborate treatment, thus making a greater departure from the simplicity and brevity of lyrics for musical accompaniment. Here belong such poems as Poe's "Raven," Francis Thompson's "Hound of Heaven," Shelley's "To a Skylark," and D. G. Rossetti's "Blessed Damozel."

Reflective poetry.—Reflective poems comprise still another group. These may have considerable emotional qualities, but the emotion is restrained and is subservient to intellectual or even contemplative qualities. Here belong poems like Wordsworth's "Tintern Abbey," Longfellow's "Bells of San Blas," Emerson's "Each and All," Browning's "Abt Vogler," Matthew Arnold's "Rugby Chapel," and E. A. Robinson's "Flammonde."

The dramatic lyric.—A large body of lyric poetry is dramatic in presentation and yet does not fall in the category of dramatic poetry proper because of its method of composition and its evident subjective qualities. These usually present a definite situation and are in the form of monologues or are spoken in the first person. To such poems Browning gave the name "dramatic lyrics." Examples of this type are Browning's "Andrea del Sarto," "Fra Lippo Lippi," and "My Last Duchess," Tennyson's "Maud," and Amy Lowell's "Patterns."

The didactic lyric.—Another division, still further removed from purely lyric qualities, yet subjective in presentation, is that of didactic poetry. A didactic poem is one in which the author strives by precept or example to teach a lesson or present a view with the purpose of influencing his reader. Such are Chaucer's "Truth Shall Make You Free," Pope's "Essay on Man," A. H. Clough's "Say Not the Struggle Naught Availeth," Bryant's "Thanatopsis," Longfellow's "Psalm of Life" and "Arsenal at Springfield," Oscar Wilde's "Ballad of Reading Gaol," and Elinor Wylie's "Eagle and the Mole."

Satirical poems.—Another group, often assigned by prosodists to a category of its own co-ordinate with narrative, lyric, and dramatic poetry, but more accurately included under lyric, as expressing essentially the personal feeling of the author about some matter, person, or condition, is satirical poetry. Here the author caricatures the foibles or failings or pretensions of mankind or holds these up to ridicule. Examples are Dryden's *Absalom and Achitophel,* Pope's *Dunciad,* Burns's "To a Louse," John Trumbull's *Progress of Dulness,* and many of Lowell's *Biglow Papers.*

SUBDIVISIONS OF DRAMATIC POETRY

Since drama is a special literary form, written primarily for presentation on a stage by a group of actors and exists as poetry only incidentally, a full consideration of its forms does not come within the scope of this work. Yet some notice must be taken of it, for some of the finest poetry is found in dramas.

Drama always depicts some sort of struggle, usually between persons, but occasionally between a person and some force or set of circumstances, or between different forces within a single individual. It is developed by dialogue and is usually written for presentation on a stage through the medium of actors.

The main types of drama are tragedy, comedy, melodrama, and farce. *Tragedy* is a form of drama in which the protagonist—usually, but not always, the character known technically as the hero or heroine—is opposed by forces or circumstances which, usually because of some flaw in himself, he cannot overcome, thus leading to his frustration. *Comedy* is a form of drama in which the protagonist overcomes whatever forces oppose him and achieves that for which he struggles. *Melodrama* is a form of drama which portrays action of a highly sentimental and sensational sort, quite out of the everyday experience of the average person, and in which the chief characters achieve happiness, no matter how perilous the circumstances they have had to face, or how improbable such result would be in the light of actual experience. *Farce* is a form of drama in which is depicted improbable happenings of a highly ludicrous sort, in which absurdities abound, and in which logic of plot is subordinated to wit.

While poetry might be the medium of expression for any of these forms, actually few melodramas and farces have been written in verse. Much of the tragedy and comedy of past times, however, was written as poetry. All the great Greek dramatists—Æschylus, Sophocles, Euripides, and others—made verse their vehicle of expression. It was used almost exclusively in English drama until the age of Elizabeth, when both prose and poetry were used, some plays employing prose and others verse, while many—most of Shakespeare's, for example—made use of both prose and poetry in the same play. It has been used in drama with effect occasionally since the beginning of the seventeenth century, but when the drama has been for public presentation on a stage, poetry has largely given way to prose in recent times.

Two special instances of the use of poetry in dramatic compositions should be noted, however. One of these is the masque, a spectacular type of presentation which gained popularity in the late sixteenth and the early seventeenth centuries. The masque combined elaborate stage properties and costuming, and dance and song, with poetic dialogue and declamation. Such excellent poets as Ben Jonson, Chapman, Campion, Dekker, Ford, and Milton wrote the words for masques; and since their contribution may be thought of as a special type of dramatic poem, it belongs rather to poetry than to drama proper. The most famous example is Milton's *Comus*.

The so-called "closet drama" comprises another subdivision. A "closet drama" is a long poem, written in the manner of a drama but meant to be read rather than acted. It uses dialogue and all the usual mechanism of the ordinary stage play but lacks action or other intrinsic dramatic qualities, and its essential poetic conception or its elaborateness may render it too difficult for stage presentation. To this class belong such dramas as Shelley's *Prometheus Unbound* and Hardy's *The Dynasts*.

CHAPTER VI

RHYTHM AND METRE

STRUCTURALLY the chief distinguishing quality of poetry is rhythm. The word *rhythm* is derived from the Greek ῥυθμός, meaning *measured motion*. In a broad sense rhythm means recurrence in time, and is applicable to any wave-like motion. Hence the ancients, observing the motions of the heavenly bodies, with the consequent effects of day and night, the flow and ebb of the tides, and the return of the seasons, conceived of the universe as operating according to rhythmical laws and, pushing the analogy further, spoke of "the music of the spheres." And although the idea of the universe has changed considerably since Ptolemy's day, we still accept the principle of rhythm as immanent in nature. It is observable in our own bodies also in such matters as walking and breathing. Its universality, indeed, seems to indicate the operation of a fundamental law, the tendency of which is towards a resolution of chaos into harmony and order. In this sense it operates also in verse, tending to reduce the language of everyday speech into patterns. In the narrow sense, as rhythm applies to verse in particular, it means the recurrence of accent at fairly regular time intervals and is called *metre*.

The terms *rhythm* and *metre* are often used interchangeably, but as rhythm in a broad sense is applicable to prose and to free verse as well as to more strictly patterned language, it seems better to distinguish the two, calling metre *organized rhythm*. That is, when rhythm follows a definite pattern, so that the number of syllables between accents and the intensity of the accents are normally regular, we have metre. The elements of metre, then, are accent and time intervals, and an understanding of these will lead to an understanding of metre as the term is used in poetry.

ACCENT

By accent is meant the prominence given to one syllable over adjacent syllables. This prominence may result from one of three causes or a combination of them. The first is the rise in pitch, which is brought about by an increase in the rate of vibration producing a sound, thus rendering the sound more acute. In some languages—French, for example—pitch is the important element in accent, but in English it is of much less importance than intensity.[1] The second cause of accent is increase in quantity, by which is meant the time employed in speaking the syllable. In Greek and Latin verse, quantity—or length of syllable—was the sole principle upon which metre was based. But like pitch it is of minor importance in English poetry, for although there is a tendency in English to take longer in speaking a syllable containing a long vowel or a diphthong than one containing a short vowel, the difference is too inappreciable to form the basis of rhythm. Yet as one of the elements producing accent, although of less significance than stress, it should not be ignored. The third cause of accent is stress, by which is meant the intensity or force with which a syllable is spoken. This is the element of paramount importance in producing accent as the term is used in English. So considerable is this importance, indeed, that the term *stress* is frequently used as a synonym for the inclusive term *accent*.

The problem of the student beginning a study of prosody is not so much, however, to determine what are the elements of accent as to know where accent occurs, for it is the latter which leads to correct scansion and hence ultimately to intelligent reading. Three reasons exist for the accentuation of certain syllables in verse, and an understanding of these should lead to a correct marking of accent. The first is based on the requirement of language which demands in words of more than one syllable an accent on a certain one of the syllables. Thus in "Michigan" the laws governing pronunciation require that the first syllable be accented and the other two unaccented. This cause of accent is called *etymological*. The second reason for the occurrence of accent grows out of the importance of the word in the line and is based on the general practice of stressing important words. Such reason for accent is called *rhetorical*. The third reason for accent is based on metrical requirements. That is, the swing of the verse demands the accentuation of certain syllables or monosyllabic words which do not require accent for etymological or rhetorical reasons. This is called

[1] For an interesting attempt at a scientific comparison of French and English accent with a view to determining the chief qualities of each, see "An Experimental Study of Accent in French and English," by C. E. Parmenter and A. V. Blanc. in *Publications of the Modern Language Association*, XLVIII, 598 ff.

metrical accent. For instance, in these lines from one of Robert Bridges' sonnets:

> The very names of things beloved are dear,
> And sounds will gather beauty from their sense,

the first syllables of *very, gather,* and *beauty* and the second syllable of *beloved* are accented for etymological reasons; *names, dear, sounds,* and *sense* are accented for rhetorical reasons; and *things* and *from* for metrical reasons.

TIME INTERVALS

In addition to the occurrence of accent, a fundamental principle of metre is that these accents shall recur at fairly regular time intervals. The tendency in English verse is for the accent to recur after an interval of not fewer than one nor more than two unstressed syllables. In actual practice there are frequent modifications of this system in even the most metrical verse, while in free verse it scarcely applies at all. Yet it is so much the normal usage in all English poetry except free verse that it may be accepted as a rule.

Besides unstressed syllables as a means of designating time intervals, pauses are sometimes used. In such instances, for example, as

> Should auld acquaintance be forgot,
> And auld lang syne?

and

> London bridge is falling down,
> My fair lady,

pauses instead of unstressed syllables fill the time intervals in the second line of each. When this is done the stressed syllables are usually lengthened also to help compensate for the lack of intervening unstressed syllables.

Cesura.—Another type of pause does not take the place of omitted syllables but helps to divide longer lines of poetry—usually lines of eight or more syllables—into natural speech units. Such a break in the rhythm is called *cesura* and is normally coincident with rhetorical pause in a line. In the older poetry cesura was a normal element of verse, but in the poetry of recent periods it is frequently omitted, or when it is used, great liberty is taken in placing it. In verse containing five stresses to the line, the normal place of cesura is after the second or third stress, in lines of six stresses after the third, and of seven stresses after the fourth, although there are frequent modifications of this practice. Here are some examples, with the cesura marked by a vertical line. Five-stress verse:

> The mind is its own place, | and in itself
> Can make a Heaven of Hell, | a Hell of Heaven.
> —MILTON, *Paradise Lost*, I

Six-stress verse:

> Somewhat apart from the village, | and nearer the Basin of Minas,
> Benedict Bellefontaine, | the wealthiest farmer of Grand-Pré,
> Dwelt on his goodly acres; | and with him, directing his household,
> Gentle Evangeline lived, | his child, and the pride of the village.
> —LONGFELLOW, *Evangeline*, I

Seven-stress verse:

> There's not a joy the world can give | like that it takes away,
> When the glow of early thought declines | in feeling's dull decay.
> —BYRON, "Stanzas for Music"

Eight-stress verse:

> Then, methought, the air grew denser, | perfumed from an unseen censer,
> Swung by Seraphim | whose foot-falls tinkled on the tufted floor.
> —POE, "The Raven"

When the cesura occurs after a stressed syllable, as in the quotation from *Paradise Lost,* it is called *masculine;* and when after an unstressed syllable, as in the first line of the quotation from *Evangeline,* it is called *feminine.*

This chapter has dealt only with the general problem of accent and time intervals; the following chapter considers these in a more particular way.

CHAPTER VII

THE FOOT AND THE LINE

POETRY is organized on the basis of the line.[1] An explanation of the metre of a poem is made, therefore, in terms of the line. To describe a line of poetry one should (1) name the basic foot, (2) tell how many feet are in the line, (3) note any substitution for a basic foot, (4) report any excess or defect of unstressed syllables at the beginning or end of a line, (5) tell the type of final stress, (6) note the position of the cesura when it occurs, and (7) tell whether the line is "end-stopped" or "run-on."

BASIC FEET

The foot, which is the unit used in measuring a line of poetry, consists of a group of syllables arranged according to a definite pattern. In English poetry the foot contains either two or three syllables, one—and only one—of which is accented (except in the spondaic foot and the pyrrhic foot, which are used only as substitute, never as basic feet). The foot receives its name from the number of syllables it contains and the position of the accented syllable. In English prosody four principal feet are recognized— the iamb, the trochee, the anapest, and the dactyl.

An iambic foot, or an iamb, is one composed of two syllables with the accent on the second (e.g., Detroit, infer).[2]

A trochaic foot, or a trochee, is one composed of two syllables with the accent on the first (e.g., Boston, accent).

An anapestic foot, or an anapest, is one composed of three syllables with the accent on the third (e.g., employee).

---

[1] In prosody the technical term for a line is *verse,* from the Latin *versus,* from *vertere,* to turn round. The popular use of *verse* for an organized group of lines is therefore incorrect, the proper term for the latter being *stanza;* but since *verse* is also used in this book for a certain class of metrical composition, the term *line* will be employed instead of the technical term.

[2] In this book an accented syllable is marked thus (') and an unaccented one thus (x), because the marks more commonly used, (-) for an accented and (ᴗ) for an unaccented syllable, although correct in classic poetry where the versification is based on long and short syllables, are incorrect in English verse, where length of syllable is a minor element and stress the important element (see p. 41).

[44]

A dactylic foot, or a dactyl, is one composed of three syllables with the accent on the first (e.g., Míchĭgăn, mýstĭcăl).[3]

Of these the iamb and the trochee, it will be noted, are alike in having two syllables, and the anapest and the dactyl in having three syllables; while the iamb and the anapest are alike in accenting the final syllable, and the trochee and the dactyl in accenting the first syllable. When the unaccented syllable comes first and is followed by the accented, the rhythm is called ascending; and when the accented syllable comes first, followed by the unaccented, it is called descending.[4]

The Number of Feet in a Line

These feet are usually grouped in certain definite patterns to form lines, and the lines named according to the number of feet in each. Thus when there is one foot to the line the verse is called *monometer;* when there are two feet, *dimeter;* when three feet, *trimeter;* when four feet, *tetrameter;* when five feet, *pentameter;* when six feet, *hexameter;* when seven feet, *heptameter;* when eight feet, *octometer;* and when nine feet, *nonameter.* Lines of one foot and nine feet are rare in English verse. The most common metres are tetrameter and pentameter.

Some lines, having a certain arrangement of metre and feet, have special names. Iambic tetrameter is called *long metre;* iambic tetrameter alternating with iambic trimeter, *common metre;* and iambic trimeter, *short metre.* Iambic pentameter is called *heroic metre.* An *alexandrine* is a line containing six iambic feet.

[3] In classical versification some writers distinguish a great variety of feet in addition to the four basic types described here, and some writers on English verse follow them in recognizing several additional feet. Of these, only one, the amphibrachic foot, or the amphibrach, deserves much notice. It is a foot of three syllables with the accent on the second (e.g., Chĭcágŏ, pŏlítĕnĕss), and is sometimes used to explain the metre which Browning used in "How They Brought the Good News from Ghent to Aix,"

Ĭ sprăng tó | thĕ stírrŭp, | ănd Jórĭs, | ănd hé.

Actually, however, all English rhythms are explainable on the basis of the feet already described and two substitute feet to be explained presently. Thus the line from Browning's poem may be explained as having anapestic metre with an iambic substitution in the first foot.

[4] If the student finds it difficult at first to remember these definitions, it may help him to note that the initial letters of *iambic* and *anapestic,* and of *ascending,* the term that defines this type of rhythm, are vowels, while the initial letters of *trochaic* and *dactylic,* and of *descending,* the term that defines this type, are consonants.

Substitutions for the Basic Foot

A whole poem written in perfectly regular metre—that is, with the same number of syllables in every line and with the accents recurring with absolute regularity—would become monotonous. Hence to give variation and color to his verse, the poet employs occasional, or even frequent, substitutions for the basic foot.

The most common form of substitution is that of another one of the principal feet for the dominant foot. Thus in iambic verse there may appear an occasional trochee or anapest, in trochaic verse an occasional dactyl or iamb, and so on. In addition to the interchange of principal feet, another form of substitution is the use of a spondaic or a pyrrhic foot.

A spondaic foot, or spondee, is composed of two syllables, both of which are accented (e.g., New York, wave-like).

A pyrrhic foot is composed of two syllables, neither of which is accented.[5]

From the definitions of these feet and from our knowledge that an alternation of accented and unaccented syllables is a fundamental quality of English poetry, it will appear at once that neither of these can be named the basic foot in a poem, and that their only purpose is to serve as occasional substitutions.

Excess and Defect of Unstressed Syllables at the Beginning and End of a Line

Lines like these:

> Then the little Hiawatha
> Learned of every bird its language,
> Learned their names and all their secrets,

are sufficiently described by calling them trochaic tetrameter, since there are but eight syllables to a line, of which the first in each line and alternate syllables thereafter are accented. Occasionally, however, the poet modifies the metre by adding an extra syllable at the beginning or by omitting the unstressed syllable at the end. A

---

[5] Obviously no single word can be offered to illustrate the pyrrhic foot, since every dissyllabic English word has an accent on one of the syllables. For this reason many prosodists disclaim the pyrrhic as a foot in English verse, explaining the appearance of more than two unstressed syllables between stressed ones in other ways. The pyrrhic, however, especially because it balances the spondee, serves a convenient purpose when there is need to explain the occurrence together of several unstressed syllables, and obviates the necessity of formulating a more elaborate system of versification.

variation from the typical metre by the addition of an extra unstressed syllable at the beginning of the line is called *anacrusis;* and
a variation by the omission of the final unstressed syllable is called
catalexis. Thus the line,

> Of all the beasts he learned the language,

is called trochaic tetrameter with anacrusis. And the lines,

> Not enjoyment, and not sorrow,
> Is our destined end or way,

are explained as trochaic tetrameter with catalexis in the second
line. Although catalexis means properly the omission of a *final*
unstressed syllable, it is applied loosely to the omission of initial
unstressed syllables also, as in the second of these lines:

> Maud Muller on a summer's day
> Rakes the meadow sweet with hay.

A variation from the normal metre by the addition of a final
unstressed syllable is called *feminine ending,* as in the second
couplet following:

> He spoke of the grass and flowers and trees,
> Of the singing birds and the humming bees;
>
> Then talked of the haying, and wondered whether
> The cloud in the west would bring foul weather.

TYPE OF FINAL STRESS

In metres that require an accent on the final syllable, the ending is said to be *strong* if the accented word is rhetorically important, as in the line:

> The deep Heart answered, "Weepest thou?"

and *weak* if the accent is on an unimportant word, as in the first
line of the following:

> The long day wanes, the twilight deepens, and
> The world is still and peaceful here to-night.

END-STOPPED AND RUN-ON LINES

A line is said to be "end-stopped" if the rhetorical and metrical sense concur to require a pause upon the completion of the
line, as in the following:

Our midnight is thy smile withdrawn,
Our noontide is thy gracious dawn;
Our rainbow arch thy mercy's sign;
All, save the clouds of sin, are thine!
                    —HOLMES, "A Sun-Day Hymn"

And when the rhetorical sense does not permit a pause at the end of a line so as to coincide with the metrical pause, the line is called "run-on." In the following example all the lines are "run-on":

For I have revelled, when the sun was bright
I' the summer sky, in dreams of living light
And loveliness,—have left my very heart
In climes of mine imagining, apart
From mine own home, with beings that have been
Of mine own thought.
                    —POE, "Dreams" [6]

[6] In learning to describe a line one should note that there is no relationship between the metrical scheme and the word sense. For instance, in the lines,

Behold her, single in the field,
Yon solitary Highland lass,

the metre is iambic tetrameter. The feet, therefore, consist of groups of syllables which, for the most part, are grammatically and rhetorically meaningless: behold, her sin, gle in, the field, yon sol, i tar, y high, land lass. The analogy may be somewhat far-fetched, yet there is a resemblance between the foot in verse and the measure in music. To note a further resemblance, moreover, as several measures (usually four) are combined to make a phrase—the smallest musical section that expresses a complete idea—so the poet combines several feet to form a group of words analogous to a musical phrase. These groups are so balanced that they produce a major rhythm which transcends and comprehends the elementary rhythm that we call metre. The study of *phrasing* (the combining of groups of words according to their grammatical or rhetorical sense to form a major rhythm) and of the analogy between poetic rhythm and music belongs rather to the advanced study of prosody, however, than to such an elementary study as this.

CHAPTER VIII

THE STANZA

A STANZA is a group of lines arranged as a melodic unit according to a definite pattern. Since stanzas are made by grouping lines, obviously two lines are the fewest that a stanza may contain. There is no arbitrary limit at the other extreme to the number of lines a stanza may have, although in practice stanzas of more than twelve lines are rare.

A stanza is described by giving the type of metre and the rime-scheme. In giving the rime-scheme, *a* is always used to denote the first line and all lines thereafter in the same stanza which rime with it, *b* for the next line containing a different riming word, *c* for the third, and so on.

Stanza forms are too numerous and varied to allow a description of them all. A few with special names, however, should be learned. In other instances the student will have to give detailed descriptions of individual stanzas—an easy task once he knows how to explain metre and rime-scheme.

THE COUPLET

The shortest form of the stanza is the couplet, which consists of two lines riming *aa*. Couplets may be written in any metre, but those written in iambic pentameter are somewhat more common than other metres, and to this special type is given the name *heroic couplet*. Following are some examples of the couplet:

> To draw no envy, Shakespeare, on thy name,
> Am I thus ample to thy book and fame,
>
> While I confess thy writings to be such
> As neither man nor muse can praise too much.
> > —BEN JONSON, "To . . . Shakespeare"
>
> Why did I write? what sin to me unknown
> Dipt me in ink, my parents', or my own?
>
> As yet a child, nor yet a fool to fame,
> I lisp'd in numbers, for the numbers came.
> > —POPE, "Epistle to Dr. Arbuthnot"

Yet I doubt not thro' the ages one increasing purpose runs,
And the thoughts of men are widen'd with the process of the suns.
—TENNYSON, "Locksley Hall"

THE TERCET

Stanzas of three lines are called tercets. Several variations of this form are possible, the most common being *aaa*. Others are *aab, aba,* and *abb*. Examples follow:

(*aaa*)   This truth within thy mind rehearse,
That in a boundless universe
Is boundless better, boundless worse.
—TENNYSON, "The Two Voices"

(*aab*)   Deep in my heart old longings and regret,
Though covered with cold ashes, smoulder yet,
And winds of memory fan them into flame.
—MURRY ALISON, "Persistence"

(*aba*)   Never was fairer view:
The trees and flowers were strange;
The world was fresh and new.
—ROBERT PRINCE, "New Life"

(*abb*)   I said I stood upon thy grave,
My Mother State, when last the moon
Of blossoms clomb the skies of June.
—WHITTIER, "Arisen at Last"

A special type of tercet is *terza rima*. This properly is not a stanza form in the same sense as the other types given here, since the rime-scheme is continuous. The first tercet rimes *aba,* the first and third lines of the second tercet rime with the second line of the preceding one, and so on, thus: *aba, bcb, cdc, ded,* etc. This is an Italian form, the most famous poem employing it being Dante's *Divina Commedia*. It was introduced into English by Sir Thomas Wyatt (1503-1542) in a group of satires, "On the Mean and Sure Estate," "Of the Courtier's Life," and "How to Use the Court and Himself." Although employed but rarely by English poets, its use, in a modified form, by Shelley in his "Ode to the West Wind," and by Browning in "The Statue and the Bust" gives it a sure place among English stanza forms. The following is from Browning's poem:

So! while these wait the trump of doom,
How do their spirits pass, I wonder,
Nights and days in the narrow tomb?

Still, I suppose, they sit and ponder
What a gift life was, ages ago,
Six steps out of the chapel yonder.

Only they see not God, I know,
Nor all that chivalry of His,
The soldier-saints who, row on row,

Burn upward each to his point of bliss—
Since, the end of life being manifest,
He had burned his way through the world to this.

THE QUATRAIN

Stanzas of four lines, the most common of all stanza forms,
are called *quatrains*. The most common forms are *abab, abcb,* and
abba, although such other combinations occur as *aaaa, aabb, aaab,
abaa, aaba,* and *abbb.* Two forms of the quatrain have special
designations: the form *abba* in iambic tetrameter is called the *In
Memoriam* stanza because Tennyson employed it with such success
in the poem of that name, although he did not invent it; and the
form *abcb* with iambic tetrameter alternating with iambic trimeter
lines is called the *ballad stanza* because of its frequent use in early
ballads. Some examples of the more common quatrains follow:

(*abab*) Love seeketh not itself to please,
        Nor for itself hath any care,
      But for another gives its ease,
        And builds a Heaven in Hell's despair.
            —W. BLAKE, "The Clod and the Pebble"

(*abcb*) There lived a wife at Usher's Well,
        And a wealthy wife was she;
      She had three stout and stalwart sons,
        And sent them o'er the sea.
            —"The Wife of Usher's Well."

I met a lady in the meads
  Full beautiful, a faery's child;
Her hair was long, her foot was light,
  And her eyes were wild.
            —KEATS, "La Belle Dame sans Merci"

[51]

(*abba*) Our little systems have their day;
     They have their day and cease to be;
     They are but broken lights of thee,
    And thou, O Lord, are more than they.
        —TENNYSON, *In Memoriam*

(*aaba*) Ah, fill the Cup:—what boots it to repeat
     How Time is slipping underneath our feet:
      Unborn To-morrow and dead Yesterday,
    Why fret about them if To-day be sweet!
        —FITZGERALD, *The Rubáiyát*

THE QUINTAIN

Stanzas of five lines, or quintains, although occurring much less frequently than quatrains, are fairly common in English poetry. A great many combinations are possible in five-line stanzas. Only a few examples of the more usual ones can be given here.[1]

(*ababa*) *Who is it that this dark night*
     Underneath my window plaineth?
     It is one who from thy sight
     Being, ah, exiled, disdaineth
     Every other vulgar light.
        —SIR PHILIP SIDNEY, "Eleventh Song"

(*ababb*) We look before and after
      And pine for what is not:
     Our sincerest laughter
      With some pain is fraught;
     Our sweetest songs are those that tell of saddest thought.
        —SHELLEY, "To a Skylark"

(*abccb*) There was a time when all mankind
     Did listen with a faith sincere
     To tuneful tongues in mystery versed;
     Then Poets fearlessly rehearsed
     The wonders of a wild career.
        —WORDSWORTH, "Peter Bell"

---

[1] A special form of the five-line stanza is the *limerick,* used for humor and burlesque. It was popularized by Edward Lear (1812-1888) in his *Book of Nonsense* (1846), and has been a favorite with writers of light verse ever since. Its rime-scheme is *aabba,* the third and fourth lines being shorter than the others. The following example from Lear's verse illustrates the form:

    There was an old person whose habits
    Induced him to feed upon rabbits;
     When he'd eaten eighteen
     He turned perfectly green,
    Upon which he relinquished those habits.

(*aabab*) My lute, awake! Perform the last
    Labor that thou and I shall waste:
      And end that I have now begun:
    And when this song is sung and past,
      My lute, be still, for I have done.
           —SIR T. WYATT, "The Unkindness of His Love"

THE SESTET

Stanzas of six lines, or sestets, are capable of dozens of separate rime-schemes and are frequent in English poetry. A few may be given by way of illustration.

(*ababab*) She walks in beauty, like the night
      Of cloudless climes and starry skies,
    And all that's best of dark and bright
      Meet in her aspect and her eyes,
    Thus mellow'd to that tender light
      Which heaven to gaudy day denies.
           —BYRON, "She Walks in Beauty"

(*ababcc*) I wandered lonely as a cloud
    That floats on high o'er vales and hills,
    When all at once I saw a crowd,
    A host, of golden daffodils;
    Beside the lake, beneath the trees,
    Fluttering and dancing in the breeze.
        —WORDSWORTH, "I Wandered Lonely as a Cloud"

(*aabccb*) O Bells of San Blas, in vain
    Ye call back the Past again!
      The Past is deaf to your prayer;
    Out of the shadows of night
    The world rolls into light;
      It is daybreak everywhere.
        —LONGFELLOW, "The Bells of San Blas"

(*abbaab*) Thus, I had so long suffered in this quest,
      Heard failure prophesied so oft, been writ
      So many times among "The Band"—to wit,
    The knights who to the Dark Tower's search addressed
    Their steps—that just to fail as they, seemed best,
      And all the doubt was now—should I be fit?
      —BROWNING, "Childe Roland to the Dark Tower Came"

THE SEVEN-LINE STANZA

The most famous type of stanza containing seven lines is that known as *rime royal*, employed by Chaucer in many of his poems, by Sackville in his part of "The Mirror for Magistrates," by Shakespeare in *The Rape of Lucrece,* and, in more recent times, by William Morris and John Masefield. Rime royal consists of seven lines of iambic pentameter, riming *ababbcc.*

> For som men seyn, if god seth al biforn,
> Ne god may not deceyved ben, pardee,
> Than moot it fallen, though men hadde it sworn,
> That purveyaunce hath seyn bifore to be.
> Wherfor I seye, that from eterne if he
> Hath wist biforn our thought eek as our deed,
> We have no free chois, as these clerkes rede.
> —CHAUCER, *Troilus and Criseyde*

A great many rime-schemes are possible in stanzas of seven lines. The student will find examples of some of these in Anne Bradstreet's "Contemplations" (*ababccc*); Philip Freneau's "Literary Importation" (*aaabbcc*); O. W. Holmes's "Chambered Nautilus" (*aabbbcc*); J. R. Lowell's "Bibliolatres (*ababccb*); Browning's "Guardian Angel" (*ababcca*); D. G. Rossetti's "Soothsay" (*aabbcca*); and Swinburne's "Appeal" (*abcabca*).

THE EIGHT-LINE STANZA

A special type of eight-line stanza that has been popular with English poets is the *ottava rima.* Like *terza rima* and the sonnet, it was introduced into English from the Italian by Sir Thomas Wyatt. It consists of eight lines of iambic pentameter, riming *ababacc.* Some English poems written in *ottava rima* are Wyatt's "Of His Love That Pricked Her Finger with a Needle," Spenser's "Virgil's Gnat," the epilogue of Milton's "Lycidas," Keats's "Isabella," Byron's *Don Juan,* Bryant's "Evening Wind," and Longfellow's "Birds of Killingworth."

> *Ave Maria!* blessed be the hour!
>   The time, the clime, the spot, where I so oft
> Have felt that moment in its fullest power
>   Sink o'er the earth so beautiful and soft,
> While swung the deep bell in the distant tower,
>   Or the faint dying day-hymn stole aloft.
> And not a breath crept through the rosy air,
> And yet the forest leaves seem'd stirr'd with prayer.
> —BYRON, *Don Juan,* III, 102

The eight-line stanza, or octave, is probably next to the quatrain the most common stanzaic form in English poetry.   The most common arrangement is to double the quatrain, with such rime-schemes resulting as *ababab*, *ababcdcd*, *abcbdefe*, *abbaabba*, and *abbacddc*, as in E. C. Pinkney's "A Health," Stephen Foster's "My Old Kentucky Home," Emerson's "Sphinx," Poe's "Haunted Palace" and "Conqueror Worm," Joaquin Miller's "Columbus," and E. A. Robinson's "For a Dead Lady."   Another method is to combine four couplets to form the octave, as in J. W. Riley's "When the Frost Is on the Punkin."   Other forms of this stanza are *ababccdd*, as in R. H. Wilde's "My Life Is Like the Summer Rose," and *aaabcccb*, as in Longfellow's "Skeleton in Armor."

THE NINE-LINE STANZA

The most famous of nine-line stanzas is that invented by the Elizabethan poet, Edmund Spenser, and used by him in *The Faerie Queene*.   It is called the *Spenserian stanza* in honor of its inventor. It consists of eight lines of iambic pentameter and a final line of iambic hexameter, with the rime-scheme *ababbcbcc*.   It has been a popular form with English poets since the revival of interest in Spenser about the middle of the eighteenth century.   Some of those employing it are James Thomson in "The Castle of Indolence," Burns in "The Cotter's Saturday Night," Byron in "Childe Harold's Pilgrimage," Keats in "The Eve of St. Agnes," Shelley in "The Revolt of Islam" and "Adonais," Tennyson in "The Lotos-Eaters," J. R. Drake in "To a Friend," and Joaquin Miller in "Exodus for Oregon."   The following examples will suffice to illustrate the form:

> These three on men all gracious gifts bestow,
> Which decke the body or adorne the mynde,
> To make them lovely or well favoured show,
> As comely carriage, entertainment kynde,
> Sweet semblaunt, friendly offices that bynde,
> And all the complements of curtesie:
> They teach us, how to each degree and kynde
> We should ourselves demeane, to low, to hie;
> To friends, to foes, which skill men call Civility.
> —SPENSER, *The Faerie Queene*, VI, x, 23

> Most musical of mourners, weep anew!
> Not all to that bright station dared to climb;
> And happier they their happiness who knew,
> Whose tapers yet burn through that night of time

In which suns perished; others more sublime,
Struck by the envious wrath of man or god,
Have sunk, extinct in their refulgent prime;
And some yet live, treading the thorny road,
Which leads, through toil and hate, to Fame's serene abode.
                                        —SHELLEY, "Adonais"

Examples of nine-line stanzas other than the Spenserian are Bryant's "June" (*ababccbdd*), Longfellow's "My Lost Youth" (*abaabcddc*), Whittier's "Memories" (*abaabcdcd*), J. R. Lowell's "To a Dandelion" (*ababaccdd*) and "Jonathan to John" (*ababc-dede*), and W. V. Moody's "Gloucester Moors" (*ababcdccd*).

STANZAS OF MORE THAN NINE LINES

As stated earlier in this chapter, there is no limit upward as to the number of lines a stanza may have. Many poems written in stanzas of ten, twelve, and even more lines may be found, but the arrangement of lines is so diverse and the number of poems having such long stanzaic forms comparatively so few that a list would be fruitless. A good exercise for the student would be to turn through some collection of poetry and make a list of all poems with more than nine lines to a stanza, noting the rime-scheme of each.

STANZAS WITH REFRAIN AND TAIL-RIME

Refrain stanzas are those in which the final line, or several lines, of each stanza is repeated throughout the poem. The following examples illustrate the usage:

> I that in heill was and gladness
> Am trublit now with great sickness
> And feblit with infirmitie:—
> *Timor Mortis conturbat me.*
> —W. DUNBAR, "Lament for the Makers"

> Forget not yet the tried intent
> Of such a truth as I have meant;
> My great travail so gladly spent,
> Forget not yet!
> —SIR T. WYATT, "Forget Not Yet"

> The twentieth year is well-nigh past
> Since first our sky was overcast;
> Ah, would that this might be the last!
> My Mary!
> —W. COWPER, "My Mary"

Somewhat back from the village street
Stands the old-fashioned country-seat.
Across its antique portico
Tall poplar-trees their shadows throw;
And from its station in the hall
An ancient timepiece says to all,—
    "Forever—never!
    Never—forever!"
—LONGFELLOW, "The Old Clock on the Stairs"

A *tail-rime stanza* is one in which two short lines rime together, serving as "tails" to the different parts of the stanza, as in the following:

Love is sickness full of woes,
    All remedies refusing;
A plant that with most cutting grows,
    Most barren with best using.
        Why so?
More we enjoy it, more it dies;
If not enjoyed, it sighing cries,
        Hey ho.
      —SAMUEL DANIEL, "Love"

The mossy marbles rest
On the lips that he has prest
    In their bloom,
And the names he loved to hear
Have been carved for many a year
    On the tomb.
      —O. W. HOLMES, "The Last Leaf"

CHAPTER IX

COMPLEX FORMS APPLYING TO WHOLE POEMS

THE SONNET

THE sonnet is a poem of fourteen lines, written in iambic pentameter, with a special rime-scheme. Two forms exist in English poetry—the Italian and the English. The Italian form, an imitation of the Italian sonnet of the thirteenth to sixteenth centuries, consists of an octave and a sestet, riming in the octave *abbaabba* and in the sestet *cdecde* or *cdcdcd* or infrequently in some other manner. The English form (sometimes called the Shakespearean, because Shakespeare employed this form when writing his famous sonnet-sequence) consists of three quatrains and a couplet, riming *abab cdcd efef gg*.[1]

The origin of the sonnet has not been traced. Some believe it to have originated with the Provençal poets; others insist that it was in Italy before it was in Provence; still others think it was an Arabic form and entered Italy through Sicily as a result of the latter's contact with Saracen culture. Whatever its ultimate source, it appears as a recognized form in Italy by the middle of the thirteenth cenutry. Such famous poets as Dante, Petrarch, Tasso, Ariosto, and Michael Angelo wrote sonnets, and in the early part of the sixteenth century Sir Thomas Wyatt, who had come in contact with Italian poetry while on ambassadorial missions for Henry VIII, introduced the sonnet to England. He did not, however, observe very closely the regulations governing the rime-scheme as practiced by the Italian poets, his greatest departure from the normal Italian form being to close his sonnets with a couplet, a practice not found in Italian poetry.[2] Henry Howard, Earl of Surrey (1515-1547), one of Wyatt's friends and admirers, varied from the Italian type still further and produced what is called the English form of the sonnet. The Elizabethan sonneteers—the

---

[1] A variation of the English form is that employed by Edmund Spenser (1552-1599) in which the rime-scheme is *abab bcbc cdcd ee*. This so-called Spenserian sonnet never became popular with English poets and is scarcely found outside of Spenser's poetry.

[2] See Charles Tomlinson, *The Sonnet, Its Origin, Structure, and Place in Poetry*, 1874 ed., p. 38.

most famous of whom were Sir Philip Sidney, Samuel Daniel, Henry Constable, Michael Drayton, Spenser, and Shakespeare— followed the form invented by Surrey; and it was not until well along in the seventeenth century, when Milton, an able student of Italian, based his sonnets on Italian models, that the Italian form was followed closely in English. Few sonnets were written in English between 1658, the date of Milton's last one, and the middle of the eighteenth century, when Joseph and Thomas Warton wrote sonnets. In 1789 William Lisle Bowles (1762-1850) published *Fourteen Sonnets,* which influenced Coleridge and his contemporaries and helped bring about a revival of interest in the sonnet. Nearly all the Romantic poets wrote sonnets, but by far the best sonneteers of the group were Wordsworth and Keats. Except for Keats, however, who followed the Italian models in the majority of his sonnets, they used the form with considerable looseness. During the latter part of the nineteenth century, a serious study of the sonnet began, and various books appeared dealing with its history and structure, while rules were laid down for its correct formation.[3] These resulted in more care being devoted to the form, with the consequent elimination of much of the looseness of structure which marked the sonnets of the majority of writers before 1850.[4]

A *sonnet-sequence,* or sonnet cycle, is a group of sonnets having a common theme or addressed to a single individual, and usually dealing with love. The Italian poet Petrarch (1304-1374) with his famous cycle to Laura was chiefly responsible for the popularity of the sonnet-sequence in England towards the close of the sixteenth century. Some of the more important Elizabethan sonnet-sequences are Sir Philip Sidney's *Astrophel and Stella,* Spenser's *Amoretti,* Samuel Daniel's *Delia,* Michael Drayton's *Idea,* and Shakespeare's unnamed sequence. More recent ones are Mrs. Browning's *Sonnets from the Portuguese,* D. G. Rossetti's *House of Life,* Robert Bridges' *Growth of Love,* W. E. Leonard's *Two Lives,* and Edna Millay's *Fatal Interview.*

[3] Important among these were the following: Leigh Hunt and S. A. Lee, *The Book of the Sonnet,* 1867; C. Tomlinson, *The Sonnet, Its Origin, Structure, and Place in Poetry,* 1874; Hall Caine, *Sonnets of Three Centuries,* 1882; W. Sharp, *Sonnets of This Century,* 1886.

[4] In strict usage the Italian sonnet requires a rhetorical pause at the end of the octave, the first eight lines stating a general proposition or idea, which ascends to a climax at the end of the second quatrain, and the last six proceeding to a conclusion. In English practice, however, this usage has been rarely followed. For a full discussion of the matter see Tomlinson, *The Sonnet, Its Origin, Structure, and Place in Poetry,* pp. 27-8, and W. J. Courthope, *History of English Poetry,* II, 91.

The following examples will serve to illustrate the various forms as employed in English poetry.

The Italian form as modified by Wyatt:

> The pillar perish'd is whereto I leant,
> The strongest stay of mine unquiet mind;
> The like of it no man again can find,
> From east to west still seeking though he went,
> To mine unhap. For hap away hath rent
> Of all my joy the very bark and rind:
> And I, alas, by chance am thus assign'd
> Daily to mourn, till death do it relent.
> But since that thus it is by destiny,
> What can I more but have a woful heart;
> My pen is plaint, my voice is careful cry,
> My mind is woe, my body full of smart;
>   And I myself, myself always to hate,
>   Till dreadful death do ease my doleful state.
>   —Sir T. Wyatt, "The Lover Laments the
>   Death of His Love"

The English form invented by Surrey:

> The soote season, that bud and bloom forth brings,
> With green hath clad the hill, and eke the vale:
> The nightingale with feathers new she sings;
> The turtle to her mate hath told her tale;
> Summer is come, for every spray now springs,
> The hart hath hung his old head on the pale;
> The buck in brake his winter coat he flings;
> The fishes flete with new repaired scale;
> The adder all her slough away she slings;
> The swift swallow pursueth the flies smale;
> The busy bee her honey now she mings;
> Winter is worn that was the flowers' bale.
>   And thus I see among these pleasant things
>   Each care decays, and yet my sorrow springs!
>   —Surrey, "Description of Spring'

The Spenserian adaptation of the English form:

> Fresh Spring, the herald of loves mighty king,
> In whose cote-armor richly are displayd
> All sorts of flowers, the which on earth do spring,
> In goodly colors gloriously arrayd;
> Goe to my love, where she is carelesse layd,

Yet in her winters bowre not well awake;
Tell her the joyous time wil not be staid,
Unlesse she doe him by the forelock take;
Bid her therefore her selfe soone ready make,
To wayt on Love amongst his lovely crew;
Where every one, that misseth then her make,
Shall be by him amearst with penance dew.
    Make hast, therefore, sweet love, whilest it is prime;
    For none can call againe the passed time.
—SPENSER. Amoretti, LXX

The English sonnet in the hands of Shakespeare:

When in the chronicle of wasted time
I see descriptions of the fairest wights,
And beauty making beautiful old rime,
In praise of ladies dead and lovely knights,
Then, in the blazon of sweet beauty's best,
Of hand, of foot, of lip, of eye, of brow,
I see their antique pen would have expressed
Even such a beauty as you master now.
So all their praises are but prophecies
Of this our time, all you prefiguring;
And, for they looked but with divining eyes,
They had not skill enough your worth to sing:
    For we, which now behold these present days,
    Have eyes to wonder, but lack tongues to praise.
—SHAKESPEARE, Sonnets, CVI

The Italian sonnet as used by Milton:

When I consider how my light is spent
Ere half my days in this dark world and wide,
And that one talent which is death to hide
Lodged with me useless, though my soul more bent
To serve therewith my Maker, and present
My true account, lest He returning chide,
"Doth God exact day-labor, light denied?"
I fondly ask. But Patience, to prevent
That murmur, soon replies, "God doth not need
Either man's work or his own gifts. Who best
Bear his mild yoke, they serve him best. His state
Is kingly: thousands at his bidding speed,
And post o'er land and ocean without rest;
They also serve who only stand and wait."
—MILTON, "On His Blindness"

The Wordsworthian adaptation of the Italian sonnet:

> It is a beauteous evening, calm and free,
> The holy time is quiet as a Nun
> Breathless with adoration; the broad sun
> Is sinking down in its tranquillity;
> The gentleness of heaven broods o'er the Sea:
> Listen! the mighty Being is awake,
> And doth with his eternal motion make
> A sound like thunder—everlastingly.
> Dear Child! dear Girl! that walkest with me here,
> If thou appear untouched by solemn thought,
> Thy nature is not therefore less divine:
> Thou liest in Abraham's bosom all the year;
> And worshipp'st at the Temple's inner shrine,
> God being with thee when we know it not.
>
> —WORDSWORTH, "To His Daughter, Caroline"

The Italian form as used by Keats:

> Much have I travell'd in the realms of gold,
> And many goodly states and kingdoms seen;
> Round many western islands have I been
> Which bards in fealty to Apollo hold.
> Oft of one wide expanse had I been told
> That deep-brow'd Homer ruled as his demesne;
> Yet did I never breathe its pure serene
> Till I heard Chapman speak out loud and bold:
> Then felt I like some watcher of the skies
> When a new planet swims into his ken;
> Or like stout Cortez when with eagle eyes
> He star'd at the Pacific—and all his men
> Look'd at each other with a wild surmise—
> Silent, upon a peak in Darien.
>
> —KEATS, "On First Looking into Chapman's Homer"

The Italian form in the Victorian period:

> How do I love thee? Let me count the ways.
> I love thee to the depth and breadth and height
> My soul can reach, when feeling out of sight
> For the ends of Being and ideal Grace.
> I love thee to the level of everyday's
> Most quiet need, by sun and candle-light.
> I love thee freely, as men strive for Right;
> I love thee purely, as they turn from Praise.

I love thee with the passion put to use
In my old griefs, and with my childhood's faith.
I love thee with a love I seemed to lose
With my lost saints—I love thee with the breath,
Smiles, tears, of all my life!—and, if God choose,
I shall but love thee better after death.
—MRS. BROWNING, *Sonnets from the Portuguese*, XLIII

THE ODE

The ode is defined in Webster's *New International Dictionary* as "a poem characterized by sustained nobility of sentiment and appropriate dignity of style"; in the *Century Dictionary* as "a lyric poem expressive of exalted or enthusiastic emotion, especially one of complex or irregular metrical form"; and by Sir Edmund Gosse in *English Odes* as "any strain of enthusiastic and exalted lyrical verse, directed to a fixed purpose, and dealing progressively with one dignified theme." These definitions, so comprehensive as to be of little aid to a student in attempting to distinguish the ode, are the result of an effort to reconcile under one head poems essentially different in structure. As a matter of fact the ode exists in three forms in English poetry—the *regular* or *Pindaric* ode, the *irregular* or *Cowleyan* ode, and the *Horatian* ode—and between two of the forms at least there is as much difference as between the sonnet and the ode. For a proper understanding of the ode, one needs to know something of its origin and history.

The Pindaric ode.—The ode originated in Greece and was a name applied to a poem arranged for musical accompaniment (the term is from ᾠδή, from ἀείδειν, to sing). All Greek songs were classified in two groups: to one belonged those expressing the personal utterance of the poet, and to the other, those written to be sung by a chorus of dancers. The poems of both groups were called odes, but the former, developed by such lyricists as Alcæus, Sappho, and Anacreon were much like the modern lyric of ordinary stanzaic form, while the latter, in the hands of poets like Alcman, Stesichorus, Simonides, Bacchylides, and Pindar, were based on elaborate and formal metrical schemes and were considerably different from the ordinary lyric. Of the poets in the latter group the name of Pindar (522-443 B.C.) has been most closely associated with the ode. He wrote his odes for various public occasions, particularly for commemorations of victories at the great games, and developed an elaborate form for them. As he constructed the ode, it consisted of several parts, each part having three subdivisions, conforming to different movements of the chorus—the strophe, or turn, which was sung while the chorus was moving in one direction from the right to the left of the altar; the antistrophe, or counter-turn, an exact duplicate of the strophe, which was sung while the chorus was making the counter movement to its original position; and the epode, or stand, which was sung while the chorus was stationary. Within each part, the strophe and antistrophe were alike in structure, and the epode different; and each part, consisting of strophe, antistrophe, and epode, exactly duplicated the others—that is, if an ode had three parts, parts two and three would have the same structure as part one, the six strophes and antistrophes having exact stanzaic forms, and the three epodes being alike but different from the strophes and antistrophes. This will be clearer by an illustration, for which purpose an ode by Thomas Gray (1716-1771), who used the Pindaric form with great skill, is given.

I, 1

Awake, Æolian lyre, awake,
And give to rapture all thy trembling strings.
From Helicon's harmonious springs
   A thousand rills their mazy progress take:
The laughing flowers that round them blow,
Drink life and fragrance as they flow.
Now the rich stream of music winds along,
Deep, majestic, smooth, and strong,
Thro' verdant vales, and Ceres' golden reign:
Now rolling down the steep amain,
Headlong, impetuous, see it pour;
The rocks and nodding groves rebellow to the roar.

I, 2

Oh! Sov'reign of the willing soul,
Parent of sweet and solemn-breathing airs,
Enchanting shell! the sullen Cares
   And frantic Passions hear thy soft control.
On Thracia's hills the Lord of War
Has curb'd the fury of his car,
And dropt his thirsty lance at thy command.
Perching on the scept'red hand
Of Jove, thy magic lulls the feather'd king
With ruffled plumes and flagging wing:
Quench'd in dark clouds of slumber lie
The terror of his beak, and lightnings of his eye.

I, 3

Thee the voice, the dance, obey,
Temper'd to thy warbled lay.
O'er Idalia's velvet-green
The rosy-crownèd Loves are seen
On Cytherea's day;
With antic Sport, and blue-eyed Pleasures,
Frisking light in frolic measures;
Now pursuing, now retreating,
    Now in circling troops they meet:
To brisk notes in cadence beating,
    Glance their many-twinkling feet.
Slow melting strains their Queen's approach declare:
    Where'er she turns, the Graces homage pay.
With arms sublime, that float upon the air,
    In gliding state she wins her easy way:
O'er her warm cheek, and rising bosom, move
The bloom of young Desire and purple light of Love.

II, 1

Man's feeble race what ills await!
Labor, and Penury, the racks of Pain,
Disease, and Sorrow's weeping train,
    And Death, sad refuge from the storms of fate!
The fond complaint, my song, disprove,
And justify the laws of Jove.
Say, has he giv'n in vain the heav'nly Muse?
Night and all her sickly dews,
Her spectres wan, and birds of boding cry,
He gives to range the dreary sky;
Till down the eastern cliffs afar
Hyperion's march they spy, and glitt'ring shafts of war.

II, 2

In climes beyond the solar road,
Where shaggy forms o'er ice-built mountains roam,
The Muse has broke the twilight gloom
    To cheer the shivering native's dull abode.
And oft, beneath the od'rous shade
Of Chili's boundless forests laid,
She deigns to hear the savage youth repeat,
In loose numbers wildly sweet,
Their feather-cinctur'd chiefs, and dusky loves.

Her track, where'er the goddess roves,
Glory pursue, and gen'rous Shame,
Th' unconquerable Mind, and freedom's holy flame.

II, 3

Woods, that wave o'er Delphi's steep,
Isles, that crown th' Ægean deep,
Fields, that cool Ilissus laves,
Or where Mæander's amber waves
In lingering lab'rinths creep,
How do your tuneful echoes languish,
Mute, but to the voice of anguish!
Where each old poetic mountain
   Inspiration breath'd around;
Ev'ry shade and hallow'd fountain
   Murmur'd deep a solemn sound:
Till the sad Nine, in Greece's evil hour,
   Left their Parnassus for the Latian plains.
Alike they scorn the pomp of tyrant Power,
   And coward Vice, that revels in her chains.
When Latium had her lofty spirit lost,
They sought, O Albion! next thy sea-encircled coast.

III, 1

   Far from the sun and summer-gale,
In thy green lap was Nature's Darling laid,
What time, where lucid Avon stray'd,
   To him the mighty mother did unveil
Her awful face: the dauntless child
Stretch'd forth his little arms and smil'd.
"This pencil take (she said), whose colors clear
Richly paint the vernal year:
Thine too these golden keys, immortal Boy!
This can unlock the gates of joy;
Of horror that, and thrilling fears,
Or ope the sacred source of sympathetic tears."

III, 2

   Nor second He, that rode sublime
Upon the seraph-wings of Ecstasy,
The secrets of th' abyss to spy.
   He pass'd the flaming bounds of place and time:

The living throne, the sapphire blaze,
Where angels tremble while they gaze,
He saw; but, blasted with excess of light,
Clos'd his eyes in endless night.
Behold, where Dryden's less presumptuous car,
Wide o'er the fields of glory bear
Two coursers of ethereal race,
With necks in thunder cloth'd, and long-resounding pace.

III, 3

Hark, his hands the lyre explore!
Bright-eyed Fancy, hov'ring o'er,
Scatters from her pictur'd urn
Thoughts that breathe, and words that burn.
But ah! 'tis heard no more—
Oh! lyre divine, what daring spirit
Wakes thee now?   Tho' he inherit
Nor the pride, nor ample pinion,
    That the Theban eagle bear,
Sailing with supreme dominion
    Thro' the azure deep of air:
Yet oft before his infant eyes would run
    Such forms as glitter in the Muse's ray,
With orient hues, unborrow'd of the sun:
    Yet shall he mount, and keep his distant way
Beyond the limits of a vulgar fate,
Beneath the Good how far—but far above the Great.
                              —"The Progress of Poesy"

This ode contains three parts. It is written in iambic metre (with catalexis in some of the lines in the epode), and the rime-scheme of the first strophe is $a^4b^5b^4a^5c^4c^4d^5d^4e^5e^4f^4f^6$, of the antistrophe the same, and of the epode, $a^4a^4b^4b^4a^3c^4c^4d^4e^4d^4e^4f^5g^5f^5g^5h^5h^6$; the second strophe and antistrophe are identical in structure with the first, and the second epode with the first epode; and the third part is identical in structure with the two preceding parts.

The number of parts an ode might have was flexible, but each part had to be complete with strophe, antistrophe, and epode. A special stanzaic form common to all odes was not demanded, and Pindar and others who developed the formal ode were accustomed to exercise their ingenuity by inventing for different odes individual metrical schemes.

But not in form only did Pindar influence the ode. He helped also to give it a grand manner and a dignified and exalted subject matter. For this there were two reasons. The first lay in the use made of the formal ode. Since it was presented by a chorus upon great occasions, it could contain nothing mean and vulgar; and since it was usually in praise of the gods or of some hero or of the victors in the great games, its manner was exalted and its style dignified. The second reason lay with the poet himself. Pindar was noted for his high seriousness, for his piety towards the gods, and for the noble and pure style of his verse, and these qualities came to be associated with the form which he distinguished.

The first regular, or Pindaric, ode in English was by Ben Jonson (1572-1637), "To Sir Lucius Cary and Sir H. Morison." In the eighteenth century William Congreve (1670-1729) revived interest in the form, and in his *Discourse on the Pindarique Ode* (1706) was the first to call attention to the principles upon which the true Pindaric ode is based. But because of its intricacy of structure and the fact that its chief *raison d'être,* to furnish words for a dancing chorus on a formal occasion, does not exist in English, it has never been popular with English poets, and since Gray has fallen into disuse.

The Horatian ode.—Among Latin poets the ode took an entirely different form from that developed by Pindar and his group. It has already been noted that the Greeks applied the term to all poems written to be sung—to the personal utterances of such poets as Alcæus, Anacreon, and Sappho as well as to the poems of Bacchylides and Pindar. The Latin poets Catullus (*c.* 84-54 B.C.) and Horace (65-8 B.C.) were greatly influenced by the former group, not only finding inspiration in the themes used by this group, but applying to their own poems the term which the Greek lyricists used to designate their personal utterances. These *odes* had ordinary stanzaic forms, were personal in tone, were in fact in no sense different from any other ordinary lyric. Under the influence of these Latin poets, particularly of Horace, many English poets have designated as odes poems which are like any other lyric poem in form and subject matter. Such odes are called *Horatian.* Examples are Ben Jonson's "Ode to Himself"; William Collins's "Ode to Evening" and "Ode to Simplicity"; Thomas Gray's "Ode on a Distant Prospect of Eton College" and "Ode on the Death of a Favorite Cat Drowned in a Tub of Gold Fishes"; Wordsworth's "Ode to Duty"; Shelley's "Ode to the West Wind"; Keats's "Ode to a Nightingale" and "Ode on a Grecian Urn"; and Emerson's "Ode Sung in the Town Hall, Concord."

The irregular, or Cowleyan, ode.—Another type of ode, now usually called the *irregular*, or *Cowleyan*, ode but at the time called a *Pindarique*, came into vogue during the seventeenth century through the influence of Abraham Cowley (1618-1667). While an exile in France about 1650, with the only book at hand a text of Pindar's poems, Cowley came under the spell of the Greek poet and began to write odes in what he thought was Pindar's manner; but he misconceived the form of Pindar's odes, and instead of using the formal metrical scheme which Pindar employed, with its exactly arranged divisions, he employed a very irregular metrical scheme with no formal relationship between the various divisions, with long and short lines intermixed without plan, and with a rime-scheme without pattern. But since this form gave poets much greater freedom than they were accustomed to when employing the usual stanza forms, it became for a time highly popular after the publication by Cowley of his volume, *Pindarique Odes* (1656). After Congreve's *Discourse on the Pindarique Ode*, with the consequent greater understanding of the true Pindaric, the Cowleyan ode lost favor, but was revived by the Romantic poets, and in such poems as Wordsworth's "Ode on the Intimations of Immortality," Coleridge's "Ode to the Departing Year," and Shelley's "Ode to Naples" reached its zenith. Later good examples of the form are Tennyson's "Ode on the Death of the Duke of Wellington," J. R. Lowell's "Ode Recited at the Harvard Commemoration," and W. V. Moody's "Ode in Time of Hesitation."

To allow the student to compare the Cowleyan ode with the strict Pindaric form, as typified by Gray in the example on page 64, a part of Wordsworth's ode is given:

I

There was a time when meadow, grove, and stream,
The earth, and every common sight,
    To me did seem
  Apparelled in celestial light,
The glory and the freshness of a dream.
It is not now as it hath been of yore;—
  Turn wheresoe'er I may,
    By night or day,
The things which I have seen I now can see no more.

II

The rainbow comes and goes,
    And lovely is the rose,
    The moon doth with delight
Look round her when the heavens are bare,
    Waters on a starry night
    Are beautiful and fair;
The sunshine is a glorious birth;
But yet I know, where'er I go,
That there hath passed away a glory from the earth.

III

Now, while the birds thus sing a joyous song,
    And while the young lambs bound
        As to the tabor's sound,
To me alone there came a thought of grief:
A timely utterance gave that thought relief,
        And I again am strong:
The cataracts blow their trumpets from the steep;
No more shall grief of mine the season wrong;
I hear the echoes through the mountains throng,
The winds come to me from the fields of sleep,
        And all the earth is gay;
            Land and sea
    Give themselves up to jollity,
        And with the heart of May
    Doth every beast keep holiday;—
        Thou Child of Joy
Shout round me, let me hear thy shouts, thou happy Shepherd-boy!

IV

Ye blessed Creatures, I have heard the call
    Ye to each other make; I see
The heavens laugh with you in your jubilee;
    My heart is at your festival,
    My head hath its coronal,
The fulness of your bliss, I feel—I feel it all.
        Oh, evil day! if I were sullen
        While Earth herself is adorning,
            This sweet May-morning,
        And the children are culling
            On every side,
        In a thousand valleys far and wide,

Fresh flowers; while the sun shines warm,
And the Babe leaps up on his Mother's arm:—
I hear, I hear, with joy I hear!
—But there's a Tree, of many, one,
A single Field which I have looked upon,
Both of them speak of something that is gone:
The pansy at my feet
Doth the same tale repeat:
Whither is fled the visionary gleam?
Where is it now, the glory and the dream?

V

Our birth is but a sleep and a forgetting:
The Soul that rises with us, our life's Star,
Hath had elsewhere its setting,
And cometh from afar:
Not in entire forgetfulness,
And not in utter nakedness,
But trailing clouds of glory do we come
From God, who is our home:
Heaven lies about us in our infancy!
Shades of the prison-house begin to close
Upon the growing boy,
But he beholds the light, and whence it flows,
He sees it in his joy;
The youth, who daily farther from the east
Must travel, still is Nature's Priest,
And by the vision splendid
Is on his way attended;
At length the man perceives it die away,
And fade into the light of common day.

VI

Earth fills her lap with pleasures of her own;
Yearnings she hath in her own natural kind,
And, even with something of a Mother's mind,
And no unworthy aim,
The homely Nurse doth all she can
To make her Foster-child, her Inmate Man,
Forget the glories he hath known,
And that imperial palace whence he came.

—From "Intimations of Immortality from
Recollections of Early Childhood"

FRENCH FORMS

Medieval Provençal poets invented a number of forms of considerable intricacy which had some vogue among English poets of Chaucer's time and for a while after, but then went out of use until the later Victorian age, when they were reintroduced by some of the minor poets. Since the poetry written in these forms is of minor consequence, only sufficient notice of them need be taken to allow the student to recognize them.

The ballade.—The ballade as usually written contains three stanzas of eight lines with an envoy of four lines, the stanzas riming *ababbcbc* and the envoy *bcbc*. The rimes in all stanzas are the same but with the riming words different; the final line of each stanza and of the envoy is the same. Chaucer, however, wrote ballades with stanzas of seven lines, and there are modern instances of nine-, ten-, and eleven-line stanzas, the most common, apart from the eight-line stanza, being that of ten lines with an envoy of five lines. The following example illustrates the normal type:

> There's a joy without canker or cark,
> There's a pleasure eternally new,
> 'Tis to gloat on the glaze and the mark
> Of China that's ancient and blue;
> Unchipped, all the centuries through
> It has passed, since the chime of it rang,
> And they fashioned it, figure and hue,
> In the reign of the Emperor Hwang.
>
> These dragons (their tails, you remark,
> Into bunches of gillyflowers grew)—
> When Noah came out of the ark,
> Did these lie in wait for his crew?
> They snorted, they snapped, and they slew,
> They were mighty of fin and of fang,
> And their portraits Celestials drew
> In the reign of the Emperor Hwang.
>
> Here's a pot with a cot in a park,
> In a park where the peach-blossoms blew;
> Where the lovers eloped in the dark,
> Lived, died, and were changed into two
> Bright birds that eternally flew
> Through the boughs of the may, as they sang;
> 'Tis a tale was undoubtedly true
> In the reign of the Emperor Hwang.

Envoy

Come, snarl at my ecstasies, do!
Kind critic, your "tongue has a tang";
But—a sage never heeded a shrew
In the reign of the Emperor Hwang.
                    —Andrew Lang, "Ballade of Blue China"

The *double ballade* has six stanzas of eight or ten lines, the eight-line stanza having three rimes, and the ten-line stanza, four rimes. The *ballade à double refrain* uses two refrains, one occurring as the fourth line of each stanza and the other as the eighth, and the first being repeated as the second line of the envoy and the second as the fourth line. Still another form is the *Chant Royal*, which has five stanzas of eleven lines, riming *ababccddede,* with an envoy *ddede.* These exceptional forms, however, are rare in English poetry.

The villanelle.—The villanelle consists of nineteen lines, with only two rimes, and with the first line repeated as the sixth, twelfth, and eighteenth, and the third line repeated as the ninth, fifteenth, and nineteenth. There are six stanzas, all having three lines save the last, which has four. The tercets rime *aba* and the quatrain *abaa.* A good example is Austin Dobson's "When I Saw You Last, Rose":

When I saw you last, Rose,
    You were only so high;—
How fast the time goes!

Like a bud ere it blows,
    You just peeped at the sky,
When I saw you last, Rose!

Now your petals unclose,
    Now your May-time is nigh;—
How fast the time goes!

And a life—how it grows!
    You were scarcely so shy
When I saw you last, Rose!

In your bosom it shows
    There's a guest on the sly;
(How fast the time goes!)

[73]

Is it Cupid? Who knows!
 Yet you used not to sigh,
When I saw you last, Rose;—
How fast the time goes!

The rondel and the rondeau.—*Rondel* was the old French form of *rondeau*, but in modern usage there is some difference between the forms. They are short poems, usually of thirteen or fourteen lines, with only two rimes, and requiring a certain type of refrain.

The rondel has fourteen lines, the first two being repeated as the seventh and eighth and again as the thirteenth and the fourteenth. Letting capitals stand for the repeated lines, the rime-scheme is *ABba abAB abbaAB*. There are variations, however, the fourteenth line being omitted at times, and the rime-scheme being varied, the most common variation being *ABab baAB ababAB*. The following rondel represents the normal usage:

Clipped is Fancy's wing;
 She flies for me no more
 As in the days of yore
When first I learned to sing.

Although to rime I cling,
 And her sweet help implore,
Clipped is Fancy's wing;
 She flies for me no more.

Some song I fain would bring
 From love's rich, golden store
 To one whom I adore.
But ah, the bitter sting!
Clipped is Fancy's wing;
 She flies for me no more.
    —ROBERT HERNE, "Clipped Is Fancy's Wing"

The rondeau has thirteen lines and a refrain, consisting of the first half of the first line, which is repeated after the eighth and the thirteenth lines. The rime-scheme is usually *aabba aabr aabbar* (*r* standing for *refrain*), although as in the rondel there are variations from this. The lines commonly, but not invariably, have eight syllables.

With song and lute the former man
Did plead with his disdainful Ann:
   He sang of love and woe and care;
   With sighs, heartfelt, he filled the air;
Love her he would for all life's span.

"Ah, smile on me," his pleading ran;
"Cold heart, relent; recall your ban,
   I pray from lonely castle stair
          With song and lute."

But now love has another plan:
With powder, rouge, and seaside tan
   The maid, no longer lady fair,
   Pursues the man (no matter where
He seeks to hide) in her sedan,
          With song and lute."
        —EDWIN CASADY, "The Lute and the Radio"

A variation of the rondeau is the *roundel,* invented by Swinburne. It has nine lines with a refrain after the third and ninth lines. The rime is *abar bab abar*. The following is Swinburne's "Envoi" to his *Century of Roundels:*

Fly, white butterflies, out to sea,
Frail pale wings for the winds to try,
Small white wings that we scarce can see
   Fly.

Here and there may a chance-caught eye
Note in a score of you twain or three
Brighter or darker of tinge or dye.

Some fly light as a laugh of glee,
Some fly soft as a low long sigh:
All to the haven where each would be,
   Fly.

The triolet.—The triolet consists of eight lines, riming *ABaA-abAB,* the first line being repeated as the fourth and seventh, and the second line as the eighth.

All women born are so perverse
No man need boast their love possessing.
If nought seem better, nothing's worse:
All women born are so perverse.

From Adam's wife, that proved a curse
Though God had meant her for a blessing,
All women born are so perverse
No man need boast their love possessing.
                    —ROBERT BRIDGES, "Triolet"

The sestina.—The sestina, invented by the troubadour, Arnaut
Daniel (d. 1199), has six six-line stanzas and a tercet. There is
no rime, but the final words of the first stanza recur in each of the
other stanzas, and are arranged according to the following intri-
cate system: *abcdef, faebdc, cfdabe, ecbfad, deacfb, bdfeca.* In the
tercet all six words are used, one in the middle of the line and one
at the end, in this order: *b-e, d-c, f-a.* The earliest example of the
sestina in English was one by Edmund Gosse, published in 1877,
and beginning, "In fair Provence, the land of lute and rose."

CHAPTER X

POETRY WITHOUT RIME AND STANZA

BLANK VERSE

BLANK verse is iambic pentameter unrimed. It was introduced into English in the fourth decade of the sixteenth century by Henry Howard, Earl of Surrey, who used the form in translating two books of Virgil's *Aeneid*. He received the idea for blank verse from Italian poetry, where it had been introduced a few years earlier by Gian Giorgio Trissino (1478-1550) and Giovanni Rucellai (1475-1525), who experimented in omitting rime in decasyllabic verse, a type popular from the tenth century. After Surrey, blank verse was written by Nicholas Grimald (1519-1562), and by Sackville and Norton, who in 1552 produced the tragedy *Gorboduc* in this form. A few years later John Lyly and George Peele experimented with it in some of their dramas, but it was Christopher Marlowe who first showed how effective it could be as a vehicle of dramatic expression. The majesty and dignity of Marlowe's lines doubtless led to its adoption by Shakespeare, who used it in all his great dramas. Shakespeare freed it from a too narrow dependence on syllabication, gave it variety and ease, and gained for it a popularity that insured its continued use by English poets. Among his successors who employed it effectively in their dramas were George Chapman, John Webster, and John Ford; but others—particularly John Fletcher, Thomas Middleton, and James Shirley— used it with such freedom—employing substitutions, overflow syllables at the end of lines, and the like—as to make it lose something of its grandeur and dignity and assume the colloquial quality of prose. By the close of the theatres in 1642 it was being supplanted by prose.

The next great impulse in the development of blank verse was at the hands of Milton, who used it in writing his great epic, *Paradise Lost*. He recaptured its grandeur and sonorousness, and used it with a serene assurance that has given it perhaps first place among English verse-forms. Certainly the best English poetry is the blank verse of Shakespeare and Milton. Since Milton's day virtually all of the great English poets, as well as a host of minor ones, have employed blank verse in some of their work. Among the more important of these are Dryden, in the latter part of the seventeenth century; Thomson and Young in the eighteenth century; Wordsworth, Coleridge, Shelley, and Keats in the Romantic period; Tennyson, Browning, Matthew Arnold, and Swinburne in the Victorian period; and Thomas Hardy, W. B. Yeats, and Alfred Noyes in our own time. Of the American poets, Bryant wrote a very considerable part of his poetry in blank verse, and Emerson and Whittier used it occasionally; among twentieth-century poets, E. A. Robinson and Robert Frost have used the form with high skill.

A few examples will suffice to illustrate the use of blank verse from its introduction by Surrey to recent times.

> "Here lurks some craft. Good Trojans, give no trust
> Unto this horse; for, whatsoever it be,
> I dread the Greeks; yea! when they offer gifts."
> And with that word, with all his force a dart
> He lancèd then into that crooked womb;
> Which trembling stuck, and shook within the side:
> Wherewith the caves gan hollowly resound.
> And, but for Fates, and for our blind forecast,
> The Greeks' device and guile had he descried;
> Troy yet had stand, and Priam's towers so high.
> —SURREY, Tr. of the *Aeneid*, Book II

> Was this the face that launched a thousand ships,
> And burnt the topless towers of Ilium?
> Sweet Helen, make me immortal with a kiss.
> Her lips suck forth my soul; see where it flies!
> Come, Helen, come, give me my soul again.
> Here will I dwell, for Heaven is in these lips,
> And all is dross that is not Helena.
> I will be Paris, and for love of thee,
> Instead of Troy, shall Wertenberg be sacked;
> And I will combat with weak Menelaus,
> And wear thy colors on my plumèd crest:
> Yea, I will wound Achilles in the heel,
> And then return to Helen for a kiss.
> —MARLOWE, *Dr. Faustus*, xiii, 93-105

> It is the cause, it is the cause, my soul;
> Let me not name it to you, you chaste stars!

It is the cause. Yet I'll not shed her blood,
Nor scar that whiter skin of hers than snow,
And smooth as monumental alabaster.
Yet she must die, else she'll betray more men.
Put out the light, and then put out the light:
If I quench thee, thou flaming minister,
I can again thy former light restore,
Should I repent me; but once put out thy light,
Thou cunning'st pattern of excelling nature,
I know not where is that Promethean heat
That can thy light relume. When I have pluck'd the rose,
I cannot give it vital growth again,
It needs must wither: I'll smell it on the tree.
—SHAKESPEARE, Othello, V, ii, 1-15

Of Man's first disobedience, and the fruit
Of that forbidden tree whose mortal taste
Brought death into the World, and all our woe,
With loss of Eden, till one greater Man
Restore us, and regain the blissful Seat,
Sing, Heavenly Muse, that, on the secret top
Of Oreb, or of Sinai, didst inspire
That Shepherd who first taught the chosen seed
In the beginning how the heavens and earth
Rose out of Chaos: or, if Sion hill
Delight thee more, and Siloa's brook that flowed
Fast by the oracle of God, I thence
Invoke thy aid to my adventrous song,
That with no middle flight intends to soar
Above the Aonian mount, while it pursues
Things unattempted yet in prose or rhyme.
—MILTON, Paradise Lost, I, 1-16

Dust as we are, the immortal spirit grows
Like harmony in music; there is a dark
Inscrutable workmanship that reconciles
Discordant elements, makes them cling together
In one society. How strange that all
The terrors, pains, and early miseries,
Regrets, vexations, lassitudes interfused
Within my mind, should e'er have borne a part,
And that a needful part, in making up
The calm existence that is mine when I
Am worthy of myself! Praise to the end!
—WORDSWORTH, The Prelude, I, 340-350

And slowly answer'd Arthur from the barge:
"The old order changeth, yielding place to new,
And God fulfils himself in many ways,
Lest one good custom should corrupt the world.
Comfort thyself: what comfort is in me?
I have lived my life, and that which I have done
May He within himself make pure! but thou,
If thou shouldst never see my face again,
Pray for my soul. More things are wrought by prayer
Than this world dreams of. Wherefore, let thy voice
Rise like a fountain for me night and day. . . .
But now farewell. I am going a long way
With these thou seëst—if indeed I go
(For all my mind is clouded with a doubt)—
To the island valley of Avilion;
Where falls not hail, or rain, or any snow,
Nor ever wind blows loudly; but it lies
Deep-meadow'd, happy, fair with orchard lawns
And bowery hollows crown'd with summer sea,
Where I will heal me of my grievous wound."
                    —TENNYSON, "The Passing of Arthur"

FREE VERSE

Free verse is poetry of irregular metre and usually without
rime. The lines conform rather to rhetorical than to metrical
grouping. They are of varying length, a line of two feet, for instance, being followed perhaps by one of six, then nine, then three,
and so on. In addition to irregularity in the matter of length, the
lines are made up of varying types of feet within the line. Efforts
to scan free verse, in fact, lead nowhere, as one line may have
iambs, trochees, spondees, and anapests, or any other combination
of feet. The idea behind free verse is to free poetry of conformity
to what is sometimes thought to be the artificialities of the formal
metrical schemes. It is based on rhythm, but rhythm in a broad
rather than a narrow sense.[1] There is the rhythm of a clock ticking or of a metronome and of the sea beating on a rocky coast; of
the beating of a tom-tom and of the movement of air currents. The
rhythm of metrical poetry tends to approximate the ticking of the
clock and the beating of the tom-tom, while the rhythm of free
verse is more like that of waves coming in to shore. Walt Whitman, who did much to develop and popularize free verse, indeed,

[1] See p. 40.

claimed to have conceived the idea for his rhythms from listening to the beating of the surf on Long Island, where he spent his boyhood.

Yet although free verse does not depend on metre or, usually, rime, it employs all the other elements of tone quality. Good free verse, in fact, because it discards certain poetic principles, has all the more need for making use of others if it is to escape the charge of being simply prose broken up into irregular line lengths. And except in rare instances—as in the worst of Whitman's efforts, which are merely catalogued lists of things flashing through his mind, and like nothing quite so much as the index of a Sears and Roebuck catalogue—an analysis of free verse will show a greater dependence on tone color than is true of much of the more metrical poetry.

Free verse is often spoken of by partisans of the older metrical forms as if it were a sport in the garden of poetry, or as if it originated in the eccentricity of Whitman and the late-nineteenth-century French *vers-libristes* who were influenced by him. Neither view is tenable, for although it received a great impulse from Whitman, poems were written in the form long before Whitman's time, and poets who owed nothing to Whitman's influence were utilizing the form simultaneously with him. Nor did it begin in the accidental whim of some certain poet. The fact is that the germ of free verse was all the while inherent in two of the older forms—blank verse and the irregular ode—for the former lacked rime and the latter had an irregular metrical scheme, and a combination of these two elements at any time would have produced free verse. That such a combination was inevitable in the development of English poetry may be seen in experiments at least as early as Milton. In his great poem, *Samson Agonistes,* Milton used a mixture of blank verse and a very loose form which has been explained as an imitation of the Greek choral ode, but which today would assuredly be called free verse. Before the close of the eighteenth century, William Blake (1757-1827) had written considerable free verse, and Shelley's earliest work, *Queen Mab* (1812), was largely in this form. Other nineteenth-century English poets employing the form were Robert Southey, Matthew Arnold, and W. E. Henley.

In all probability if it had not been for Whitman free verse would have developed in such a normal and orderly manner that its place in poetry would have come to be accepted without question, as that of blank verse had been earlier. But Whitman's *Leaves of Grass* (first published in 1855 and expanded thereafter) aroused all the controversial instincts of adherents of the older poetry and precipitated a quarrel that raged throughout the latter part of the nineteenth century and well into the twentieth. Those who denounced Whitman's poetry were probably moved as much by his unconventional subject matter as by his form, and this confusion of matter with manner helped obscure the issue upon the outcome of which depended the future of free verse. But as a more unconventional age—or one conventional in a different way—has come to accept Whitman's ideas without shock, so it has become reconciled to the form he chose in which to express his ideas. In recent years chief hindrances to the final acceptance of free verse as a legitimate form of poetry have come from its own proponents, the first being the militant attitude of little groups who were determined to battle for free verse long after the need to battle was over, and the second being the hurt done by poetasters who, having no taste in poetry of whatever sort, saw in free verse a chance to exercise license rather than freedom, and whose compositions would have damaged any form they chose, whether prose, rimed poetry, or free verse. But with the passing of time the qualities which constitute good free verse have been recognized, the militant controversialists have tended to disappear, the work of poetasters employing this form has been discounted in the same way as if they had written sonnets or ballades, without damning the form because of those using it, and among thoughtful students of poetry free verse is recognized as a standard poetic form, by no means likely to supplant the older forms, but useful in supplementing them. Regular rhythms, metres, and rime are too firmly entrenched to be displanted; and because of the pleasure they give, they will continue to constitute the bulk of poetry; but there will probably be no time hereafter when free verse will not be written. Under certain circumstances and in the hands of a master it offers a freedom, not unwed with beauty, that the older forms do not possess. It has enriched poetry without taking away any of the values of the older forms.

Among poets of our own time who have used the form with skill are Edgar Lee Masters, Amy Lowell, Carl Sandburg, Vachel Lindsay, Ezra Pound, Hilda Doolittle, and John Gould Fletcher. They have written poor poems in free verse, just as Herrick and Wordsworth and Keats wrote poor ones in the older metrical forms, but such poems as Masters's "Lucinda Matlock," "Pauline Barrett," and "Starved Rock"; Sandburg's "Prairie," "Prayers of Steel," and "Washington Monument by Night"; Amy Lowell's

"Patterns" and "Purple Grackles"; Pound's "A Virginal" and "Night Litany"; and Fletcher's "The Grand Canyon of the Colorado" and "Lincoln," to mention but one here and there, belong to the best traditions of English poetry.

Some older examples of free verse follow; for more recent ones, the student may consult any recent anthology.

> This, this is he; softly a while;
> Let us not break in upon him.
> O change beyond report, thought, or belief!
> See how he lies at random, carelessly diffused,
> With languished head unpropt,
> As one past hope, abandoned,
> And by himself given over,
> In slavish habit, ill-fitted weeds
> O'er-worn and soiled.
> Or do my eyes misrepresent?   Can this be he,
> That heroic, that renowned,
> Irresistible Samson? whom, unarmed,
> No strength of man, or fiercest wild beast, could withstand;
> Who tore the lion as the lion tears the kid;
> Ran on embattled armies clad in iron,
> And, weaponless himself,
> Made arms ridiculous, useless the forgery
> Of brazen shield and spear, the hammered cuirass,
> Chalybean-tempered steel, and frock of mail
> Adamantean proof.
> —MILTON, *Samson Agonistes*

> Forth flew the arrows of pestilence
> Round the pale-living corse on the tree.
>
> For in Urizen's slumbers of abstraction,
> In the infinite ages of eternity:
> When his nerves of joy melted and flowed
> A white lake on the dark blue air,
> In perturbed pain and dismal torment
> Now stretching out, now swift conglobing.
>
> Effluvia vapored above
> In noxious clouds: these hovered thick
> Over the disorganized immortal,
> Till petrific pain scurfed o'er the lakes
> As the bones of man, solid and dark.
>
> The clouds of disease hovered wide
> Around the immortal in torment.

Perching around the hurtling bones,
Disease on disease, shape on shape,
Winged, screaming in blood and torment.

The eternal prophet beat on his anvils,
Enraged in the desolate darkness;
He forged nets of iron around,
And Los threw them around the bones.

The shapes, screaming, fluttered vain;
Some combined into muscles and glands,
Some organs for craving and lust.
Most remained on the tormented void—
Urizen's army of horrors.

Round the pale living corse on the tree
Forty years flew the arrows of pestilence.

Wailing, and terror, and woe
Ran through all his dismal world.
Forty years all his sons and daughters
Felt their skulls harden. Then Asia
Arose in the pendulous deep.

They reptilize upon the earth.

Fuzon groaned on the tree.
> —WILLIAM BLAKE, *The Book of Ahania*, IV

How wonderful is Death,
Death and his brother Sleep!
One, pale as yonder waning moon
With lips of lurid blue;
The other, rosy as the morn
When throned on ocean's wave
It blushes o'er the world:
Yet both so passing wonderful!

Hath then the gloomy Power
Whose reign is in the tainted sepulchres
Seized on her sinless soul?
Must then that peerless form
Which love and admiration cannot view
Without a beating heart, those azure veins
Which steal like streams along a field of snow,
That lovely outline, which is fair

As breathing marble, perish?
Must putrefaction's breath
Leave nothing of this heavenly sight
But loathsomeness and ruin?
Spare nothing but a gloomy theme,
On which the lightest heart might moralize?
Or is it only a sweet slumber
Stealing o'er sensation,
Which the breath of roseate morning
Chaseth into darkness?
Will Ianthe wake again,
And give that faithful bosom joy
Whose sleepless spirit waits to catch
Light, life, and rapture from her smile?
                              —SHELLEY, *Queen Mab*, I

Hark! ah, the nightingale—
The tawny-throated!
Hark, from that moonlit cedar what a burst!
What triumph! hark!—what pain!

O wanderer from a Grecian shore,
Still, after many years, in distant lands,
Still nourishing in thy bewildered brain
That wild, unquenched, deep-sunken, old-world pain—·
Say, will it never heal?
And can this fragrant lawn
With its cool trees, and night,
And the sweet, tranquil Thames,
And moonshine, and the dew,
To thy racked heart and brain
Afford no balm?
                    —MATTHEW ARNOLD, "Philomela"·

Poets to come! orators, singers, musicians to come!
Not to-day is to justify me and answer what I am for,
But you, a new brood, native, athletic, continental, greater than before
     known,
Arouse! for you must justify me.

I myself but write one or two indicative words for the future,
I but advance a moment only to wheel and hurry back in the darkness.

I am a man who, sauntering along without fully stopping, turns a casual
     look upon you and then averts his face,
Leaving it to you to prove and define it,
Expecting the main things from you.
                         —WHITMAN, "Poets to Come"

[85]

BIBLIOGRAPHY

FOR those who wish to pursue the study of poetry beyond an elementary text, this list is appended. It is not exhaustive, but suggestive. Many of the books listed here have bibliographies of their own.

ON THE POET AND POETRY IN GENERAL

The earliest important critical work which has influenced Western literature is Aristotle's *Poetics,* a good edition being *Aristotle's Theory of Poetry and Fine Art,* by S. H. Butcher, 1911. The first important critical works on English poetry were written in the Elizabethan period, important ones being George Gascoigne's "Certain Notes of Instruction," prefixed to his *Poesies,* 1575; Sir Philip Sidney's *Defence of Poesy,* 1595; and Samuel Daniel's *Defence of Ryme,* 1603. Wordsworth, in the Preface to *Lyrical Ballads,* 1800 (later revised and enlarged), gave a new impulse to the study of the poetic gift and was followed by others who wrote provocatively on the subject, among them Coleridge in *Biographia Literaria,* 1817; William Hazlitt in *Lectures on the English Poets,* particularly in the essay "On Poetry in General," 1818; John Ruskin in *Modern Painters,* 1843-1860; Leigh Hunt in *Imagination and Fancy,* 1844; Emerson in "Poetry and Imagination" in *Letters and Social Aims,* 1875; and Matthew Arnold in *Essays in Criticism,* Second Series, 1888. T. Ribot's *Essay on the Creative Imagination,* translated by A. H. N. Baron, 1906, is interesting as an early effort by a psychologist to explain the poetic process. Recent books of importance are Conrad Aiken's *Scepticisms,* 1919; Max Eastman's *Enjoyment of Poetry,* revised edition, 1921, and *Literary Mind,* 1931; F. C. Prescott's *Poetic Mind,* 1922; Lascelles Abercrombie's *Theory of Poetry,* 1924; I. A. Richards's *Principles of Literary Criticism,* 1924, and *Science and Poetry,* 1926; C. B. Tinker's *Good Estate of Poetry,* 1929; and A. E. Housman's *Name and Nature of Poetry,* 1933. For a brilliant exposition of an individual example of the poetic process, see J. L. Lowes' *Road to Xanadu,* 1927.

On the History of Poetry

The most complete and scholarly work on the history of poetry is W. J. Courthope's *History of English Poetry*, 6 vols., 1895-1910; an excellent short treatise is R. M. Alden's *English Verse*, 1903. F. B. Gummere's *Beginnings of Poetry*, 1901, is a scholarly study of the origins of poetry. A good short work for beginners is *The Winged Horse*, by J. Auslander and F. E. Hill, 1927.

On Prosody

George Saintsbury's *History of English Prosody*, 3 vols., 1906-1910, is the fullest treatment of the subject. Shorter works on prosody that are important are Sidney Lanier's *Science of English Verse*, 1880; E. C. Stedman's *Nature and Elements of Poetry*, 1892; T. S. Omond's *Study of Metre*, 1903, and *English Metrists* (a republication of two older essays), 1921; R. M. Alden's *Introduction to Poetry*, 1909; W. M. Patterson's *Rhythm of Prose*, second edition, 1917; and C. E. Andrews's *Writing and Reading of Verse*, 1918. The following volumes treat poetry in general and give some attention to prosody: Bliss Perry, *A Study of Poetry*, 1920; E. G. Moll, *The Appreciation of Poetry*, 1933.

The following volumes have to do with the history or the forms of the various kinds of poetry indicated in the titles: W. P. Ker, *Epic and Romance*, 1897; John Clark, *A History of Epic Poetry*, 1900; H. A. Guerber, *The Book of the Epic* (a foreword and a summary of the great epics), 1913; F. B. Gummere, *The Popular Ballad*, 1907; G. L. Kittredge and Helen C. Sargent, *English and Scottish Popular Ballads* (a fine selection, made from the five-volume collection by F. J. Child), 1904; Louise Pound, *Poetic Origins and the Ballad*, 1921, and *American Ballads and Songs* (a collection), 1922; J. A. Lomax, *American Ballads and Folk Songs*, 1934; W. H. French and C. B. Hale, *Middle English Metrical Romances* (a collection, with a good introduction), 1930; E. B. Reed, *English Lyrical Poetry from Its Origins to the Present Time*, 1912; F. E. Schelling, *The English Lyric*, 1913; Ernest Rhys, *Lyric Poetry*, 1913; T. W. H. Crosland, *The English Sonnet*, 1917 (for other books on the sonnet, see the note, page 59); Edmund Gosse, *English Odes*, 1881 (a collection, with an enlightening introduction); J. B. Reeves, *The Hymn as Literature*, 1924; J. A. Symonds, *Blank Verse*, 1895; Robert Bridges, *Milton's Prosody*, revised edition, 1921 (containing much valuable comment on prosody in general and on blank verse); Gleeson White, *Ballades and Rondeaus*, 1893 (a collection, with a good introductory essay); Carolyn Wells, *A Vers de Société Anthology*, 1907; Helen L. Cohen, *Lyric Forms from France: Their History and Their Use*, 1922 (an anthology with a good introduction on these forms); Amy Lowell, *Tendencies in Modern American Poetry*, 1917, and the introduction to *Can Grande's Castle*, 1918.

COLLECTIONS

One of the most popular of the older anthologies is *The Golden Treasury*, edited by Francis Palgrave, 1861. Two more recent ones are *The Oxford Book of English Verse*, edited by Sir A. T. Quiller-Couch, 1901; and *The College Book of Verse*, edited by R. M. Gay, 1927. A comprehensive collection of English and American poetry, arranged by types, is *Types of Poetry*, edited by J. Zeitlin and C. Rinaker, 1926; and a comprehensive collection of American poetry, arranged chronologically but indexed also by types, is *An Introduction to American Poetry*, edited by F. C. Prescott and G. D. Sanders, 1932. Representative collections of modern poetry, including most poets writing, are *Modern American Poetry*, fourth revised edition, 1930, and *Modern British Poetry*, third revised edition, 1930, edited by Louis Untermeyer; and *The New Poetry*, revised edition, 1932, edited by Harriet Monroe and A. C. Henderson. A collection of modern English and American poetry, limiting the authors to the more important ones and devoting considerable space to each, is *Chief Modern Poets of England and America*, revised edition, 1936, edited by G. D. Sanders and J. H. Nelson.

INDEX *

Abercrombie, Lascelles, 86
Accent, 40-42
Æschylus, 39
Aiken, Conrad, 86
Alcæus, 63, 68
Alcman, 63
Alden, R. M., 87
Alexandrine, 45
Allegory, 15, 17
Alliteration, 22-23
Allusions, 18-20
Amphibrach, 45 *n.*
Anacreon, 63, 68
Anacrusis, 47
Analogy, 17
Anapest, 44
Andrews, C. E., 87
Antithesis, 20
Apostrophe, 15, 18
Ariosto, 58
Aristotle, 86
Arnold, Matthew, *5, 37, 78, 81, 85,* 86
Ascending rhythm, 45
Assonance, 23
Auslander, J., 87

Bacchylides, 63, 68
Balanced sentence, 20
Ballad, the, 34-36
Ballade, the, 72-73
Ballade à double refrain, 73
Ballad stanza, 51
Barlow, Joel, 34
Baron, A. H. N., 86
Beauty, an element in poetry, 7-8
Bible, The, 18
Blake, William, 15, *51,* 81, *84*
Blanc, A. V., 41 *n.*
Blank verse, 77-80
Bowles, W. L., 59
Bradstreet, Anne, 54
Bridges, Robert, *8,* 35, *42,* 59, 76, 87
Browning, Elizabeth B., 59, *63*
Browning, Robert, 8, *20, 24,* 30, 37, *45 n.,*
  50, 53, 54, 78
Bryant, W. C., 11, *19,* 38, 54, 56, 78
Burns, Robert, 16, *18,* 36, 38, 55
Butcher, S. H., 86
Butler, Samuel, 34
Byron, Lord, 37, *43, 53, 54,* 55

Caine, Hall, 59 *n.*
Campion, Thomas, 36, 39
Casady, Edwin, *75*
Catalexis, 47
Catullus, 68
Cesura, 42-43
Chant Royal, 73
Chapman, George, 39, 77
Chatterton, Thomas, 35
Chaucer, Geoffrey, *24,* 38, 53, *54, 72*
Child, F. J., 87
Clark, Badger, 35
Clark, John, 87
Closet drama, 39
Clough, A. H., 38
Cohen, Helen L., 88
Coleridge, S. T., *4, 23, 27,* 35, 59, 69, 78,
  86
Collins, William, 68
Comedy, 38
Common metre, 45
Comparison, 16
Concreteness, 13-15
Congreve, William, 68, 69
Consonance, 23
Constable, Henry, 59
Couplet, the, 49
Courthope, W. J., 59 *n.,* 87
Cowley, Abraham, 69
Cowleyan ode, the, 69-71
Cowper, William, *56*
Crosland, T. W. H., 87
Cunningham, Allan, 35

Dactylic foot, the, 45
Daniel, Arnaut, 76
Daniel, Samuel, *57,* 59, 86
Dante, 50, 58
Definitions of poetry, 4-5
Dekker, Thomas, 39
Dentals, 22
Descending rhythm, 45
Dickinson, Emily, 14
Didactic lyric, the, 37
Dimeter, 45
Dobson, Austin, 73
Doolittle, Hilda, *82*
Double ballade, 73
Drake, J. R., 55
Dramatic lyric, the, 37

* Page references to poems, given under the author's name, are in italics.

[89]